THE tarot SPELLBOOK

78 WITCHY WAYS TO USE YOUR TAROT DECK FOR MAGICK & MANIFESTATION

SAM MAGDALENO

FAIR WINDS

Inspiring | Educating | Creating | Entertaining

Brimming with creative inspiration, how-to projects, and useful information to enrich your everyday life, quarto.com is a favorite destination for those pursuing their interests and passions.

First Published in 2022 by Fair Winds Press, an imprint of The Quarto Group,
100 Cummings Center, Suite 265-D, Beverly, MA 01915, USA.
T (978) 282-9590 F (978) 283-2742 Quarto.com

Fair Winds Press titles are also available at discount for retail, wholesale, promotional, and bulk purchase. For details, contact the Special Sales Manager by email at specialsales@quarto.com or by mail at The Quarto Group, Attn: Special Sales Manager, 100 Cummings Center, Suite 265-D, Beverly, MA 01915, USA.

26 25 24 23 22   1 2 3 4 5

ISBN: 978-0-7603-7708-6

Digital edition published in 2022
eISBN: 978-0-7603-7709-3

Library of Congress Cataloging-in-Publication Data is available

Design and Page Layout: Tanya Jacobson, jcbsn.co
Illustration: Tanya Jacobson, jcbsn.co

Printed in USA

For Scarlett,
may you always
believe in your
inner magick.

CONTENTS

Introduction

H EY, MAGICK BABE! I'M SO GLAD YOU'RE HERE. ARE YOU READY TO WORK WITH TAROT IN A WHOLE NEW WAY? I'M ALWAYS LOOKING FOR WAYS TO DEEPEN MY CONNECTION TO THE CARDS, AND I'M EXCITED TO SHARE WITH YOU WAYS TO WORK WITH TAROT BEYOND SPREADS AND READINGS.

The Tarot Spellbook helps you deepen your knowledge of the cards and provides ways to work with tarot in your craft. As a professional tarot reader, I know that tarot can be tricky to get comfortable with. We can read about card meanings until we're blue in the face, but when it comes time to actually take action . . . what then? It can be hard to find a clear-cut way to utilize the cards in your everyday life.

When I was beginning my journey, I found it helpful to place the cards into real-life context to become more familiar with them. Tarot is now my favorite magickal tool, in part because no matter what situation I find myself in, there's at least one card that relates and can offer wisdom and insight. And, as you'll see in *The Tarot Spellbook*, the lessons of tarot naturally lend themselves to an everyday spellbook. This book helps you translate the teachings of the cards into spells that you can use as you go through the different chapters, obstacles, and transitions of your life.

I'm so happy you've picked up this book. *The Tarot Spellbook* offers you a way to truly connect with tarot. So, grab a warm drink, cozy up on the couch with your tarot deck, and take a few deep breaths. Learning about the cards is about to get easier and a lot more fun. Let's go!

xo Sam

◆ HOW TO USE THIS BOOK ◆

Before we dive into the ways to use *The Tarot Spellbook*, let's talk about who can use it. Basically, this book is for any and every kick-ass witch who picks it up! Witches of every experience level and path can find meaning and connection within these spells.

- You do not have to be Wiccan to practice witchcraft or use this book.
- *The Tarot Spellbook* is beginner friendly. It was written to further your knowledge of tarot and help you learn.
- You do *not* have to be a tarot expert to use the cards in spellwork. Part of the intention behind including tarot cards in spellwork is to learn more about tarot as you work with the cards.

Okay, time to dive in! The spells in this book are based on the illustrations created by Pamela Colman Smith for the Rider-Waite-Smith deck, which is generally regarded as the first modern tarot deck. If you're interested in furthering your knowledge in tarot (which I suspect you are!), I encourage you to learn more about Pamela Colman Smith and her contributions to the world of art and the occult.

Here are ways you can use and work with *The Tarot Spellbook*.

To further your knowledge and connection with the cards. Tarot is tricky. I totally get it. It can be overwhelming, and there are always new nuances to learn. For me, simply reading about the cards wasn't enough to get things to stick and make sense. What helped the puzzle pieces fall into place was integrating their lessons into my witchcraft practice. Working with tarot in this more physical sense beyond card spreads gave me a deeper understanding and clearer reference points for the cards.

As . . . a spellbook! Who would have thought, right? *The Tarot Spellbook* was written to be used as an everyday spellbook, even if furthering your knowledge and connection with cards comes secondary to the spells themselves. Remember: The lessons of tarot extend to all aspects of life. There's a spell for all your basics, from the big life lessons of the major arcana to the smaller everyday workings of the minor arcana.

To take a deeper dive into a card's meaning. Do you keep drawing the same card over and over? And you've all but screamed, "But what do I *do* with this?!" Well, now you have something to do with those repeat offenders. If you're drawing the same card, it's helpful to put it into action in your craft. Enter, *The Tarot Spellbook*.

To reflect on your relationship with the card. You'll find a few journal questions to go along with each spell and tarot card. These questions help provide further introspection, reflection, and connection with your card and spell. You can write your answers in a journal or contemplate them during meditation. I recommend doing the journal questions after your spellwork is complete.

One more thing I want to note: Each spell focuses on one main aspect or lesson of the card. It is by far *not the only* aspect or lesson of each card! Tarot is so nuanced, and there are multiple lessons, insights, and nuggets of wisdom in each card. If there are aspects of a card that aren't discussed in this book but that pique your interest, I encourage you to branch out and further your knowledge. We are forever students of tarot!

PART One

MAKING MAGICK

☾

ONE OF THE GREAT THINGS ABOUT WITCHCRAFT IS THAT YOU GET TO MAKE YOUR MAGICK YOURS! EACH WITCH HAS A DIFFERENT PRACTICE, AND IT'S WORTH TAKING TIME TO FIND THE WAYS YOU'RE MOST COMFORTABLE.

Setting Up for Spellwork

It's important to take a few minutes to set up and prep before jumping right into spellwork. You'll want to settle into the energy and get clear and focused before you begin. Here are a few common ways witches set up:

Read the spell completely beforehand. It's best to go into spellcasting with a frame of reference for the steps of the spell, rather than reading them for the first time on the fly. This will give you a good idea of how much time you'll need and what will be expected of you.

Gather your supplies. There's nothing more frustrating than getting halfway through a spell and realizing you don't have the ingredients needed to finish it. (Not that I've ever been there. *cough cough*)

Find a quiet space that is free of any distractions. Spellwork takes concentration and focus so you don't lose your flow. Turn your cell phone to "do not disturb." Ask your family or roommates not to interrupt you. Settle pets into another room. Turn off the TV.

Set the mood. Gather any candles, crystals, herbs, or other belongings you'd like with you while you complete your spellwork. They don't have to be included in the official list of ingredients or tools; you're always free to add extra. Dim the lights, burn incense, or turn on music or ambient sound. Whatever helps you get into the right frame of mind for your spell!

Cleanse your space and tools. Before you begin, cleanse all tools and ingredients you plan on using and cleanse your space. This removes any old or unwanted energy that could interfere with your spellcasting.

The next page contains further details on cleansing your space.

Establish your intention. The Universe loves clarity! The clearer you can get with your intentions for the spell, the more likely your spell will be effective. For example, rather than saying, "I want to make more money this year," your intention could be, "I want to make $10,000 more than last year." With the first example, you could only make $1 more than last year, and the spell would technically still have worked, although it's unlikely that's what you meant!

Cast a circle. You don't have to cast a circle *every* time you practice magick. My rule for circle casting is that I will do it for spells that are more intricate, lengthy, or require in-depth focus. For quick hits of magick, such as saying affirmations throughout the day or doing a short energy cleanse, I do not cast a circle. I recommend casting a circle for every spell in *The Tarot Spellbook*. Like all magick, you can flavor the way you cast your circle according to your specific practice.

You can find more details about casting circles on page 14.

Cleansing Basics

There are many ways to cleanse your tools and space. Try these:

- Use a dried herbal wand, incense, or saltwater spray.

- Create sound vibration with bells, a singing bowl, or cymbals, or simply visualize a protective and cleansing light.

- If you don't have any cleansing tools, visualization will do the trick in a pinch. Visualize a bright light cleansing your space and your spellwork tools.

- To cleanse each tool or ingredient, hold your chosen cleansing method above it and say your intention. To cleanse your space, take your chosen cleansing method to the corners of the room, windows, and doorways. Say aloud your intentions to cleanse the space.

- Some examples of intention-setting language could be as simple as: "With this (chosen tool), I cleanse and purify this space." A more complex cleansing intention could sound something like, "I ask that my guides (or deities, ancestors, angels) be with me as I cleanse and purify this space. I, with this (chosen tool), release all previous energy as I prepare this space for (kind of spellwork). So it is."

CASTING A CIRCLE

In witchcraft, a circle is a safe space and barrier within which you practice magick. Cast a circle before you begin your spell, making sure that you have all necessary tools with you so you don't have to leave your circle in the middle of spellcasting. Once you have completed your spell or ritual, close your circle.

There are many ways to add your spin on casting a circle: working with deities, candles, crystals, or physical representations of the elements. Once you get the basics down, personalize circle casting to your magick practice.

Start by walking around the space where you will cast your circle to establish its physical boundaries. You can also point to the space using an athame*, wand, or even your finger.

Stand in the middle of your circle and call upon the elements to guide and assist you in your spellwork.

Begin with the East, the direction of Air. You can say something simple, such as, *I call upon the element of Air and ask that you aid me in my magick.*

Working clockwise, turn to the South and repeat this step with the element of Fire, saying, *I call upon the element of Fire, and ask that you aid me in my magick.*

Turn to the West, element of Water, and say, *I call upon the element of Water, and ask that you aid me in my magick.*

Next, turn to the North, element of Earth, and say, *I call upon the element of Earth, and ask that you aid me in my magick.*

Last, close your eyes and envision a portal from the top of your head into the expansive Universe. Say, *I call upon the element of Spirit, and ask that you aid me in my magick.*

Visualize and connect with each element as you call upon it. Envision a glowing mist rising from your circle, in whichever color you feel connected to.

Close with, *As above, so below.*

After your spellwork has been completed, close your circle beginning with the North, moving backward, and thank the elements for assisting you, moving counterclockwise this time.

Athame*

An athame is a double-edged blade or knife often used in ceremonial witchcraft. An athame is primarily used in a symbolic sense for directing and manipulating energy, rather than physically cutting something.

Magickal Timing

Each spell in this book lists an ideal time to perform it to give your spells a little cosmic power boost. Just as we choose spell ingredients based on their magickal properties, we can work with the properties of moon phases, days of the week, and time of day as well. This is by no means when the spell *has* to be done. Of course, you're free to cast spells whenever it feels best for you! But if you're able to, I recommend casting the spells according to the suggested timing to help add some extra magick.

Moon Phases

NEW MOON

Magickal properties: The new moon is the start of a new lunar cycle, a time for new beginnings and a fresh start. During this phase, the moon is recharging its batteries, gathering energy for the coming lunar cycle. The new moon is a time for reflection, to look inward, and ask yourself what you desire.

Ideal for: New beginnings in any area of your life, fresh starts, and establishing intentions

WAXING MOON

Magickal properties: The waxing moon is a phase of expansion, as the moon builds in fullness toward the full moon. This moon phase has lots of energy and movement behind it.

Ideal for: Building momentum, expansion, and growth

FULL MOON

Magickal properties: The height of the lunar cycle! Mama moon is full and shining in all of her glory. Think of the full moon as a giant cosmic spotlight: The full moon will shine its light on things that aren't working in your life and help provide that extra push to facilitate change. In its full state, this moon has the most energy behind it, so if you're working with a spell that feels extra difficult, the full moon is great to utilize for some extra cosmic oomph.

Ideal for: Release, forgiveness, and power

WANING MOON

Magickal properties: Coming after the full moon, the waning moon diminishes in size as it heads toward the end of its cycle. As the moon shrinks in size, this is a time of shedding your skin to be rebirthed in the next moon cycle as a more aligned version of yourself.

Ideal for: Banishing, removing obstacles, and psychic abilities/energies

DARK MOON

Magickal properties: The dark moon occurs one to three days before the new moon, when the moon is dark and barely visible in the sky. This is a time of rest and retreating inward before beginning a new cycle.

Ideal for: Clearing space, rest, meditation, and psychic work

Days of the Week

SUNDAY

Ruling planet: Sun

Magickal focus: Generosity, health, healing, strength, creativity, confidence, illumination, hope, success

MONDAY

Ruling planet: Moon

Magickal focus: Spirituality, intuition, intention, home, dreamwork, psychic work

TUESDAY

Ruling planet: Mars

Magickal focus: Ambition, sex, courage, passion, vitality, anger, achievement, strength

WEDNESDAY

Ruling planet: Mercury

Magickal focus: Communication, technology, knowledge, education, writing/speaking, expression, studying, memory

THURSDAY

Ruling planet: Jupiter

Magickal focus: Growth, luck, expansion, abundance, legal matters, money, influence, accomplishment, business

FRIDAY

Ruling planet: Venus

Magickal focus: Love, fertility, sex, healing, goddess work, the arts, friendship, beauty, harmony, creativity, relationships

SATURDAY

Ruling planet: Saturn

Magickal focus: Discipline, focus, drive, manifestation, family, transformation, overcoming, completion, obstacles, protection

Times of Day

SUNRISE

Magickal properties: Like a new moon brings that first bit of light after darkness, sunrise offers the breaking of a new day after night. Sunrises are often synonymous with rebirth and positive outlooks, making them a great time to implement fresh starts.

Ideal for: New beginnings, enlightenment, and blessings

MORNING

Magickal properties: Morning tends to be when the mind is most awake and alert (after coffee, of course), making it a good time to practice magick that relates to the conscious mind.

Ideal for: Clarity, leadership, and knowledge

NOON

Magickal properties: Noon sits between night and day, balanced perfectly in the middle. The sun is shining brightly, providing a boost of energy you can utilize if your spells need some extra cosmic magick.

Ideal for: Balance, amplifying energy, and spells that work with the sun's energy (e.g., health, vitality, strength)

SUNSET

Magickal properties: As sunset closes out the day, it brings closure and finality. If things aren't looking up in the moment, it also offers the hope and promise of a new day to begin again soon.

Ideal for: Endings, transition, hope, peace, and banishing

NIGHT

Magickal properties: In the night we are left in the darkness without the light of the sun to guide us; we rely more on intuition and are more perceptive to hearing our subconscious mind.

Ideal for: Dreams, emotions, and spells that work with the moon's energy (e.g., fertility, intuition, subconscious)

MIDNIGHT

Magickal properties: The time when the veil between worlds is thinnest, midnight offers connection to the paranormal and the spirit world.

Ideal for: Spiritual connection, divination, and invoking change

Sigil Magick

A sigil is a symbol with magickal meaning behind it. The term itself is derived from the Latin word "sigilli-um," meaning "seal." When you create a sigil, you combine your intention with a symbol, and you code, or seal it, it with meaning and purpose. For spellwork, sigils are used to tap into your subconscious mind and amplify your spells.

How does that work? When you assign meaning to a symbol, or sigil, it activates the subconscious mind, where the sigil can work without being interpreted by the conscious mind (which likes to throw in doubts and restrictions). If you simply write a word or phrase, your conscious mind interprets it. A sigil bypasses that and goes straight to the subconscious, allowing you to tap more deeply into your magick and intuition.

The power of a sigil lies in your subconscious through the creation of the sigil itself. For this reason, it can be quite personal. I find sigils I create to be more powerful than those created by others.

CREATING YOUR SIGIL

Like most things in witchcraft, there are various ways to create a sigil, and whichever way you choose should be the way that feels the most aligned and intentional to you. Sigils can be made from words, pictures, magick squares, runes, and various other methods. After you create your sigil, you will activate or charge it. This energizes it and imprints it into your subconscious mind, where it can get to work. Refer to these steps throughout *The Tarot Spellbook* when a spell asks you to create a sigil.

Creating a Word Sigil

Word sigils tend to be the simplest and are therefore one of the more commonly used types of sigils.

What you need:

- Paper and pen

Get clear on your intention. You can use a word or phrase, such as "pass my final science exam," or a full sentence, such as "I have passed my final science exam." When writing a full sentence, use present or past tense ("I am," "I have"), rather than future tense ("I will," "I want"). You want to be specific here, so limit each sigil you create to one intention. Write down your chosen phrase or sentence.

Cross out the vowels and duplicate letters.

Rearrange the remaining consonants into a symbol by overlapping the letters, connecting their curves and lines, and adding any flourishes, dots, or embellishments that feel aligned.

Remember, this is *your* sigil, so there's no certain way it "should" look. Give yourself the freedom and creativity to play around with your sigil before you decide on its final form.

Activating Your Sigil Through Burning

There are many ways to activate your sigil, from dancing, to chanting, to sex magick. Keeping with the theme of simple, I recommend using fire and burning your sigil. Before you burn your sigil, I recommend drawing a copy to remember and use in your spellwork.

What you need:

- Your sigil written on a piece of paper
- A lighter or matchbook
- A small cauldron or fireproof bowl

To activate your sigil through burning, hold it in both hands and focus on the sigil itself and your intention.

Light the sigil on fire and drop it into your cauldron to burn. Visualize your sigil releasing into the Universe as you continue to focus intently on it. If the flame goes out, simply relight the sigil.

Once the sigil has burned completely, bring your focus back to the present. Your sigil is now ready to be used in spellwork.

Making Magick Yours

When it comes to spellcasting, I encourage you to see the spell as a fluid guide, rather than something that is written in stone. Your magick practice is *your* magick practice. If part of a spell doesn't feel aligned for you, you are free to replace it with something that does.

You are also welcome to substitute ingredients in these spells if there's something you don't have on hand. The ingredients in each spell were chosen intentionally due to their properties and powers, so it's important to research an ingredient with similar properties if you are going to substitute one.

Speaking of spell ingredients, most of the candle spells in this book call for chime candles as the recommended candles to be used in each spell. Chime candles are ideal for spellwork because they're smaller than pillar candles and burn down completely in about two hours. Common practice is usually to complete your spell and do the related work, such as meditation, journaling, or mindful movement, while your candle continues to burn to completion.

Some of the spells in *The Tarot Spellbook* require you to write on, bury, or otherwise use the chosen tarot card. If you don't want to sacrifice the card from your deck, you can use a photocopy, printed, or hand-drawn version of the card.

Short on Time?

If you're a busy witch (who isn't?!) and want to let your candle burn all the way down but don't have two hours to spare, I'll share my favorite tip: birthday candles. You can use a birthday candle in place of a chime candle for most of the spells in *The Tarot Spellbook*, if you choose. They have a burn time of about ten minutes and are easily accessible and available in many colors. To keep a birthday candle in place during a spell, simply melt the bottom slightly with a lighter and stick it to a fire-safe plate or bowl.

The Most Important Ingredient in Any Spell

Your mind-set is the most important ingredient! While our magick tools and ingredients play a part in spellwork, mind-set plays a bigger part. If you're distracted by something you're doing because it feels off to you, the chances of your spell working will decrease. If you don't truly believe your spell will work . . . guess what? It's probably not going to work. Clear, specific intention and belief in yourself are the keys to successful spellcasting.

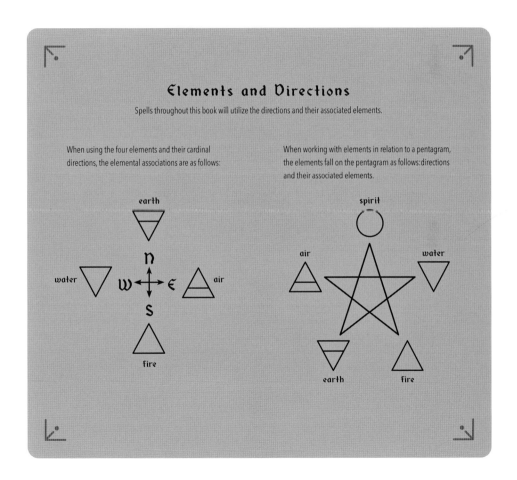

Elements and Directions

Spells throughout this book will utilize the directions and their associated elements.

When using the four elements and their cardinal directions, the elemental associations are as follows:

earth

water   n   air
w ← → e
s

fire

When working with elements in relation to a pentagram, the elements fall on the pentagram as follows:directions and their associated elements.

spirit

air   water

earth   fire

PART Two

SPELLS

☾

TIME TO SHINE UP YOUR CAULDRON AND DUST OFF YOUR TAROT DECK! NOW IS THE PART WHERE YOU WORK WITH YOUR TAROT CARDS IN A WHOLE NEW WAY: THROUGH SPELLWORK! IN THIS SECTION, YOU'LL GAIN A DEEPER UNDERSTANDING AND CONNECTION WITH YOUR TAROT CARDS BY UTILIZING THEM IN SPELLS CREATED TO HELP YOU LIVE YOUR MOST ALIGNED AND MAGICKAL AF LIFE.

The Major Arcana

THE FIRST TWENTY-TWO CARDS OF THE TAROT DECK, THE MAJOR ARCANA ENCOMPASSES SIGNIFICANT EVENTS, LESSONS, AND OBSTACLES. THE SPELLS RELATED TO THE MAJOR ARCANA ARE ONES YOU'LL LIKELY TURN TO WHEN GOING THROUGH BIG LIFE CHANGES.

The Fool

The Magician

The High Priestess

The Empress

The Emperor

The Hierophant

The Lovers

The Chariot

The Hermit

Wheel of Fortune

Justice

The Hanged Man

Death

Temperance

The Devil

The Tower

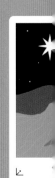

THE FOOL: Gather the Courage to Start Something New

Have you been stalling at the starting line, trying to muster up the courage to get going? The Fool encourages you to just . . . start! A card of new beginnings, The Fool is daring, carefree, and spontaneous. And the energy of The Fool is infinite! The Fool doesn't spend too much time planning things because The Fool has faith that they'll work out along the way. You know that deep in your gut, you're ready for this, babe. It terrifies you in the best way.

The Fool

A Spell Spray for New Beginnings

Timing: New moon

You're on the precipice of something great—if only you could start. In this spell, you'll work with The Fool to gather the courage to start something new.

What you need:

- Small spray bottle
- Distilled water to fill the bottle
- A few drops of rose essential oil (diluted)
- ½ teaspoon dried rosemary
- Supplies to decorate your bottle: paper, markers, stickers, etc.
- The Fool tarot card

Create your spell spray by filling your spray bottle two-thirds full with distilled water.

Add a few drops of rose essential oil, connected to the heart chakra, to inspire bravery and love. Sprinkle in dried rosemary for courage.

Decorate your bottle with words and images that connect to courage and the new "something" you're ready to start.

Close the lid and swirl the bottle clockwise three times as you visualize your new beginning.

Give yourself a little spritz and picture yourself in place of The Fool, on the precipice of something new, ready to move forward.

Charge your spell spray with the energy of The Fool by setting The Fool tarot card outside under the light of the new moon (or on a windowsill that gets moonlight) and placing your spell spray on top of it.

Retrieve your tarot card and spray the next morning and keep the spray on your altar. Spritz your heart chakra when you need a boost of courage as you take steps toward your new beginning.

JOURNAL QUESTIONS:

What could you accomplish if you let yourself begin this new journey with full trust in yourself? If you don't take risks, your life won't change: Are you okay with that? Why or why not? Whose courage do you admire? How can you embody their energy?

THE MAGICIAN: Manifest Your Desires

Wishing you could snap your fingers and make your heart's desires suddenly appear? Well, working with The Magician can't quite do that, but it's the closest thing we've got in Tarot card form. The Magician contains representations of all four suits in tarot, suggesting that everything you need is at your disposal. Like a wise mentor in a Disney movie that materializes from the mist the moment the main character is facing defeat, The Magician reminds you that you already have everything you need within you to make your dreams come true. Aww, thanks, Magician!

The Magician

An Elemental Spell to Harness Your Inner Magick

Timing: New moon, dawn

One of the great lessons of The Magician is that you don't need to *wish* for magick–*you already are the magick.* In this spell, you'll work to embody your inner magick so you can manifest your desires.

What you need:

- The Magician tarot card
- 1 bay leaf
- Pen
- Representations of Air, Fire, Water, and Earth
- Wand (can use a crystal or even your finger)

. . . .

♞ Representations of the Five Elements

Air: feather, smoke, incense, bell, fairy or angel representations, wind chime, a picture of a tornado

Fire: wand, lighter or matches, candle, cayenne pepper, a picture of the sun

Water: cup, bowl of water, moon water (see page 31), seashells, mirror, a picture of a body of water

Earth: soil, sand, crystals, acorns, seeds, sticks, a picture of mountains or a field

Spirit: angel aura crystal, clear quartz crystal, a picture of a spiral, infinity symbol, representation of a dove

. . . .

Place The Magician card in the center of your work space. Study and connect with the imagery. Can you see yourself as The Magician in your life?

Hold the bay leaf between both hands as you visualize what you're manifesting. Write your manifestation on the bay leaf and place it on top of The Magician card. In tarot, each suit corresponds with an element. For this spell, we'll be using elemental representations of the suits to work with The Magician's magick.

Hold your Air representation. Say aloud, *With Air, I see my desires clearly. Air within me, so shall it be.* Place your Air element east-facing around your bay leaf.

Hold your Fire representation. Say aloud, *With Fire, I embody passion and motivation. Fire within me, so shall it be.* Place your Fire element south-facing around your bay leaf.

Hold your Water representation. Say aloud, *With Water, I tune into and trust my intuition. Water within me, so shall it be.* Place your Water element west-facing around your bay leaf.

Hold your Earth representation. Say aloud, *With Earth, I ground my manifestations into reality. Earth within me, so shall it be.* Place your Earth element north-facing around your bay leaf.

Take your wand and charge your bay leaf with your elements by touching the wand to the leaf and each element, coming back to the bay leaf between elements.

Do this daily as you work toward your desires. You can remove The Magician card from the spell and carry it with you throughout the day, replacing it to charge with the intentions of your spell again at night.

JOURNAL QUESTIONS:

What inner power do you already possess that will help you achieve your desires? What skill can you develop to work toward your desires? What is one inspired action you can take today to work toward your desires?

THE HIGH PRIESTESS:
Strengthen Your Intuition

Sometimes in tarot readings, the cards will say, "You already know the answer, so we're keeping our lips zipped." It can be frustrating. In those readings, it's likely that The High Priestess is leading the charge! A woman of mystery and inner wisdom, The High Priestess appears when you're being asked to tap into your intuition, trust yourself, and stop seeking answers from outside sources. I mean . . . kind of rude when you're using tarot to get answers (I joke!). We love The High Priestess and her reminders to trust and listen to ourselves, even if it can be difficult at times.

The High Priestess

A Moon Magick Spell for Inner Knowing

Timing: Monday, full moon

Strengthen your intuition so you can move forward with confidence. In this spell, you'll work with The High Priestess to tap into your wise inner knowing.

What you need:

- Moonstone crystal
- Moon water (below)
- Blue or white bag or cloth
- Silver ribbon or string
- The High Priestess tarot card

Moon Water

Created by leaving water in the moonlight, moon water is a common ingredient in spells. The properties of your moon water will vary by which lunar phase the moon is in. See page 15 for information on lunar phase properties.

To make moon water, take a clear glass cup, jar, or bowl of water, and set it outside to charge in the moonlight for an hour or so before your spell. Ideally, moon water is left to charge all night, but in a pinch some moonlight is better than none! Collect your moon water and bring it inside. If you're unable to set it outside due to weather, set your water on a windowsill that gets direct moonlight.

Anoint your moonstone crystal by sprinkling the moon water on top of it with your fingers. Moonstone aids in tapping into your inner knowing and enhances your intuition, while providing comfort and a nurturing energy. Moon water contains properties that connect to the moon, which represents intuition and wisdom.

Hold the moonstone in your left palm, with your hand open, and close your eyes. Say,

High Priestess, full of mystery,
enhance my intuition as I hold this moonstone
close to me.

Ask your higher self to help guide and strengthen your intuition. If there's a certain topic you want clarity around, allow yourself to think about it, and notice how it feels in your body. Your body often reflects the inner wisdom of your intuition. Do you feel excited butterflies, or a pit in your stomach? Do your shoulders tense? Does your jaw clench? Do you feel light-headed?

Once you're finished with your meditation, place the moonstone in a blue or white bag or cloth, and tie it closed with a silver ribbon. Silver is the color associated with intuition.

Place your moonstone bag on top of The High Priestess tarot card somewhere near your bed to aid in strengthening your intuition.

When you're feeling lost or disconnected to your intuition, remove the moonstone crystal from the bag and hold it to the center of your forehead. While you take slow deep breaths, ask The High Priestess to guide you to connect to your intuition.

JOURNAL QUESTIONS:

What do intuitive nudges feel like for you? What stories have you told yourself (or been told) about why you can't or shouldn't trust you intuition? What messages has the Universe been sending you?

THE EMPRESS: Enhance Your Beauty

Key words: Abundance, beauty, fertility

The Empress is one to work with when you're feeling less than your fabulous self. As witches, we can't change our appearance by wrinkling our nose, but we can work with the magick of The Empress, a goddess-like figure of beauty, fertility, and abundance. The Empress radiates beauty from within, and she takes time to nurture others and herself. Notice the symbol for Venus on The Empress's pillow, we'll be invoking goddess Venus to work with us, as The Empress does.

The Empress

A Glamour Magick Spell to Radiate Inner Beauty

Timing: Friday

Sometimes you need an extra boost of confidence and a sprinkle of spells to feel glowy again–that's where beauty charms come in! In this spell, you'll work with The Empress to enhance your beauty.

What you need:

- Lighter or matchbook
- Red chime candle and holder
- Beauty item or accessory that gives you a boost of confidence (a lipstick or nail polish color, hair product or accessory, necklace, perfume, etc.)
- The Empress tarot card
- ¼ cup (9 g) fresh or dried rose petals

Light your red candle; the color red is associated with Venus. Invoke goddess Venus to assist in your beauty charm by saying aloud,

Goddess Venus, I ask your aid, bless this charm, and the intentions laid.

Hold your chosen item between both hands above the flame–high above the flame if it's something flammable!

Visualize or think of yourself as The Empress, wearing your chosen item: Feel the luxurious velvet of her chair, the wind kissing your cheek as it flows through the trees. Hear the rush of water from the river and the light brushing of the wheat stalks. Feel her confidence and assuredness in her power and beauty.

Set The Empress card on your altar or near your beauty or accessory products. Set your chosen item on top of The Empress. Sprinkle the rose petals around the card, circling your item with the power of self-love and peace.

Thank Venus for her aid and extinguish your candle. Leave your item there to charge with the intention and magick of The Empress.

Use your charmed item on days you need a little help feeling beautiful. Light the candle to recharge the spell and keep it lit as you get dressed, put on makeup, or take a bath, to embody the confidence of The Empress and enhance your beauty.

JOURNAL QUESTIONS:

What makes you feel beautiful? What are three qualities you possess that make you beautiful? What can you do for yourself to cultivate feeling more beautiful? This can be as simple as a weekly face mask, random act of kindness, or joyful movement of body.

THE EMPEROR: Protect Your Home

Key words: Strength, boundaries, protection

There are a few characters you don't want to f*ck with in tarot, and The Emperor is one of them. Reflecting the stubbornness of the rams associated with Aries (the astrological correspondence of The Emperor card), The Emperor is a fierce protector. Vigilant over his space and the space of those he oversees, The Emperor is stern and ambitious, yet nurturing and responsible. Wearing a suit of armor, he's ready to battle it out to defend his territory at a moment's notice. The towering mountains behind him mirror the way he safeguards those around him.

The Emperor

A Salt Spell to Protect Your Home

Timing: Tuesday

The Emperor is one to work with when you're focused on creating a safe haven, whether it's to guard against the bad vibes of your not-so-favorite neighbors or you just feel like you could use some extra protection. In this spell, you'll work with The Emperor to protect your home and those who reside in it.

What you need:

- The Emperor tarot card
- Paper and pen
- ⅓ cup (85 g) table salt
- Small shovel
- Pebbles or rocks

Place The Emperor tarot card in your pocket to embody his strength and protective energy as you work through the spell.

Using your paper and pen, create a protection sigil (see page 19) for your home. On a separate piece of paper, draw an outline of your house and draw the protection sigil inside of it.

Take the table salt and sprinkle it on top of your paper, sprinkling protection over your home.

Holding your paper with salt on it in one hand, walk the perimeter of your home, beginning at the front door and moving clockwise. Sprinkle the salt from atop your paper along the outside of your home, making sure to get corners, doorways, and windows. Visualize a strong light shield being cast over your home as you do so. While you sprinkle your salt, say aloud in a firm voice,

With strength and vigilance from my heart's center, I declare unwelcome entities no longer to enter. With this salt and spell I protect, a strong light shield around my home, and unwanted energy reject.

Once you have finished, use a small shovel to dig a hole and bury your paper and The Emperor card in your yard, near your front door, with a circle of stones surrounding it for protection. If your home doesn't have a yard space, a potted plant near your front door will also work. Repeat every year to reenergize the spell.

JOURNAL QUESTIONS:

By protecting his space, The Emperor creates safety and comfort. Do you feel comfortable in your body (your first home)? What situations or feelings come up that cause you to feel uncomfortable or unsafe? How can you invoke the protective and loving energy of The Emperor when this happens? Which of his qualities can you focus on embodying, and how?

THE HIEROPHANT: Connect with Your Ancestors

Have you ever stopped to think that you've got an entire team of ancestors rooting for you? For you to be born, you needed your parents and grandparents, eight great-grandparents, sixteen second great-grandparents, thirty-two third great-grandparents . . . and the list just keeps getting bigger! The Hierophant is a figure of authority who channels wisdom and passes on knowledge to students, reflecting the ancient knowledge and tradition passed down from our ancestors.

The Hierophant

An Altar Spell to Channel Wisdom

Timing: Night, or midnight

You'll be creating an ancestor altar and programming tools to work with to connect with your ancestors. This spell aids you in receiving and integrating their wisdom, like a student of The Hierophant.

Note: If you're adopted or don't know specific ancestors you'd like to connect with, connect to ancestors from your cultural background or in your adoptive family.

What you need:

- Altar or dedicated space
- Food offering
- Drink offering
- Lighter or matchbook
- Mugwort incense and holder
- Optional: photographs of ancestors
- Black pillar candle
- Toothpick or safety pin
- Selenite crystal
- The Hierophant tarot card

Clear a space on your altar, or create a new space dedicated to your ancestors. Set out food and drink offerings on your altar to thank and pay respects to your ancestors. These offerings can be the favorite food of a loved one, food and drink connected to your cultural heritage, or anything you're feeling a nudge to set out.

Light mugwort incense, for psychic connection. Set out photographs of your ancestors if you choose.

On a black pillar candle use a toothpick or safety pin (or desired scribing tool) to write your last name on your candle. If you have changed your last name, use your original family last name or maiden name. This is the candle you'll light whenever you wish to connect with your ancestors.

Program your selenite crystal for ancestor connection by holding it to your heart and focusing on your ancestors.

Hold the selenite crystal above the flame in one hand, and The Hierophant card over your heart space as you say,

(Last name) ancestors, I invite you here,
With love in my heart, you are forever dear.
Please be with me, knowledgeable and wise,
As I invoke you now, rise, rise, rise.

Spend some time with your ancestors. Close your eyes and receive any messages or downloads. Speak aloud to them. Ask them for their advice and guidance. Listen. What wisdom do they have to share with you?

Thank your ancestors before you leave their altar. Take extra care to note any synchronicities or signs that occur during this time, and over the next few days.

Sleep with The Hierophant tarot card and the selenite crystal under your pillow or next to your bed to receive messages from your ancestors in your dreams. Keep the food and drink offerings refreshed and light the pillar candle and work with the selenite to connect to your ancestors.

JOURNAL QUESTIONS:

What is something you have always *known* deep down? Something that feels as though it is ancient wisdom passed down? What spiritual traditions did your ancestors practice? How can you incorporate those traditions into your practice? What meaning will they hold?

THE LOVERS: Ignite Passion in Your Relationship

Key words: Love, passion, choices

Are things feeling less than flammable in your relationship lately? Time to tap into some of that fiery Lovers energy! In tarot, The Lovers is a card of romance, attraction, and passion. In the Rider-Waite-Smith version of this card, a man and woman stand naked surrounded by temptation in the form of a serpent, passion represented by fire, and what appears to be a volcano on the edge of eruption, representing, well, you know. While it is a card of romance, The Lovers is also a card of choice. The Lovers are choosing their destiny, just as in a relationship you must choose each other.

The Lovers

An Apple Magick Spell for Passion

Timing: Friday

In this spell, you'll work with The Lovers to ignite passion in your relationship. Do not perform this love spell, or any love spell for that matter, without the consent of your partner.

What you need:

- Apple half, cut from the apple around the middle
- Toothpick or safety pin
- Pinch of sugar
- Pinch of ground cinnamon
- Pinch of cayenne pepper
- Lighter or matchbook
- Red chime candle and holder
- The Lovers tarot card

The apple half represents the desire and temptation of The Lovers. Begin by holding it up near your heart center as you take three deep breaths and focus on the intention of your spell.

The seeds inside of your apple should resemble a pentagram. Using your toothpick or safety pin, carve your name on one side of the pentagram and your partner's name on the other side.

Sprinkle your sugar and spices on top of the apple, over your and your partner's names: cinnamon for success and warmth, cayenne for heat and fire, and sugar for sweetness. Taste each element on your finger before you add it to your apple, connecting with its magickal properties and feeling the texture and taste in your mouth.

Light your red candle, the flame representing passion. Hold the apple in one hand, and with the other, circle the flame over the top of the apple clockwise, drawing its energy toward you. As you do this, say aloud with each pass,

Desire and passion, hot, sticky sweet, ignite the flame in my relationship, as when The Lovers meet.

Drip some of the hot wax over the apple, sealing the ingredients over your and your lover's names. Set your apple and red candle, in a candle holder, in front of you on your altar.

As the candle burns, study The Lovers card and visualize or think about your relationship. See yourself and your partner as The Lovers in the card. What are your interactions like? What steamy fun do you get up to?

Keep your apple under your bed for two nights, on top of The Lovers card, to ignite passion in your relationship. After two nights, remove some of the seeds to use in future love spells with your partner, and compost the apple

JOURNAL QUESTIONS:

The Lovers is a card not only of passion, but also of choice. How can you choose to bring more passion into your relationship? What actions can you take? What does choosing more passion require of you? How can you show up with more naked authenticity, as The Lovers do?

THE CHARIOT: Iron Away Doubts Before a Job Interview

Key words: Determination, willpower, success

The Chariot is a card of determination, victory, and success, like when you put the pedal to the metal and charge forward at full speed, running on determination and willpower. The chariot driver takes direct action and has faith that victory is there, if only they trust in themself and hold steady in their commitment to the end goal.

The Chariot

A Glamour Magick Spell for Confidence

Timing: Waxing moon

The strength and assuredness of The Chariot is something to draw on in times of doubt or apprehension . . . and who doesn't feel that before a job interview? In this spell, you'll use your personal "chariot" to iron out all doubts so you can move forward with confidence to victory. That job is yours!

Note: This spell can also be used for meetings, performance reviews, or any big moment you want to conquer.

What you need:

- Item of clothing you will wear during your interview
- Ironing board
- Iron
- Mint essential oil (diluted)
- The Chariot tarot card

Hold your chosen item of clothing in your hands. As you do so, think about any doubts or obstacles that you're feeling fearful about regarding your interview. See all of your doubts or obstacles leaving your body and seeping into the fabric.

Place your clothing on the ironing board and turn on the iron. As it is heating up, dab diluted mint essential oil, for success and focus, on the palms of your hands.

Pick up the iron and see it as your chariot. The wrinkles and creases in your clothes are your doubts. Iron your clothing and, as you do so, visualize or think about your chariot, with you as its driver, overcoming your doubts, as with each sweep of the iron you overpower and erase them.

As you are ironing your clothing, say aloud,

With determination and iron chariot in hand,
All doubts and fears cast here are banned.
Success and victory are mine, I claim
As I wear this cloth, all others will know the same.

After you have ironed out all of your doubts (and wrinkles), run the iron over your clothing in a pentagram shape to seal the spell. Wear your clothing item with The Chariot card in your pocket during your interview to ace it!

JOURNAL QUESTIONS:

What evidence do you have that you will succeed? What have you overcome to prepare you for this moment? What driving force or motivation do you have that will never let you give up?

STRENGTH: Gain More Self-Discipline

Key words: Wisdom, beliefs, tradition

At first glance, Strength seems to be one of the more obvious cards in the major arcana of tarot. Strength represents . . . well, strength, right? Right. But! The strength expressed in the card isn't about beating Dwayne "The Rock" Johnson in an arm wrestling contest. Strength as represented in the card has tamed the lion, not with brute force, but with gentleness. She stands tall and assured, not needing to convince the lion, or anyone else, of her power. She is confident in her inner knowing. You don't need to force situations. When you believe in yourself, others will believe in you, too.

Strength

An Art Magick Spell for Self-Discipline

Timing: Sunday

Strength shows us another way of achieving our goals. In this spell, you'll work with the gentle confidence and inner power of the Strength card to gain more self-discipline.

What you need:

- Strength tarot card
- 2 pieces of paper
- Orange pen
- Handful of dirt

Begin by setting the Strength card in front of you for inspiration. Study the card and notice how gentle Strength is in her taming of the lion. Envision yourself with this loving energy as you complete the rest of the spell.

On your first piece of paper, draw a picture of a lion with your orange pen. Orange is associated with strength. It doesn't have to be gallery worthy! As long as you know what it is, that's the important part.

The lion represents your animalistic nature. Meditate or think on what you'd like to gain more discipline over; what aspect of your life are you seeking more self-control in? Inside of the lion's body, write a word or phrase signifying what it is. Really take a moment here and concentrate on this step.

On your second piece of paper, draw a picture of yourself as a divine god or goddess. Again, no judgment on how it looks! The divine figure represents the version of yourself that embodies the qualities of the Strength card: powerful and disciplined, yet gentle and kind.

Fold the lion paper three times, folding the paper away from your body, and turning it counterclockwise after each fold to banish any doubts.

Place the folded lion paper, representing what you're gaining control over, on top of your god/goddess paper, symbolizing your highest self taming the lion.

Sprinkle dirt on top to help facilitate grounding. Fold the god/goddess paper three times, enclosing it around the dirt and lion paper. Fold toward your body, and turn the paper clockwise after each fold, to draw in the energy of your god/goddess gaining control over the lion.

As you fold, say aloud,

Earth below, spirit above,
Guide me to practice self-discipline with love.
Through god/goddess energy, the wild beast I tame,
I am no longer controlled by what I do not claim.

Store your spell in a place where it won't get moved, such as inside a drawer, to facilitate its steadfast and unmovable energy. Keep the Strength card on your desk or altar as a reminder of your intentions.

JOURNAL QUESTIONS:

What is your relationship to self-discipline? How can you be kinder to yourself, using less force and more inner confidence, as you work toward change? List three reasons you're a strong, badass witch.

THE HERMIT: Quiet Your Mind

Key words: Introspection, retreat, soul searching

The Hermit is a card of wisdom and knowledge, the kind that can only be found through solo soul searching. They walk their path alone, with only the lantern of their inner light to guide the way. The Hermit finds solace in quality alone time, where they can quiet their mind. In a way, this reflects some of the reasons we pick up tarot cards: to find a moment for reflection and introspection. The Hermit asks you to carve out moments for yourself . . . and that's what we will do!

The Hermit

A Bath Magick Spell for Introspection

Timing: Dark moon, night

How many times a day do you wish for a moment of peace to help sort out the thoughts in your mind? In this spell, you'll create a retreat for yourself and work with The Hermit's energy to quiet your mind.

What you need:

- Bath
- 2 cups (448 g) Epsom salts
- A few drops of lavender essential oil (diluted)
- Lighter or matchbook
- White chime candle and holder
- Paper and pen
- The Hermit tarot card
- Cauldron or small fireproof bowl

Draw a warm bath and sprinkle in the Epsom salts, symbolizing the snowcapped mountains and also representing the grounding of Earth energy. Create a circle with the salt inside the bath to symbolize protection and sacred space. Add a few drops of lavender essential oil for relaxation.

Once inside the bath, light your white candle, representing The Hermit's lantern and your inner guiding light. As you carefully hold the candle, consider your guiding light; what keeps you moving forward and helps navigate your way?

Set the candle in its holder. Hold your pen over it and say aloud,

Inner light guiding me,
Banish the noise and let peace be.
Lantern bright and Hermit wise,
A quiet mind therein lies.

Take the pen to paper and write whatever comes to mind: things you're overthinking, or just general brain chatter. Get it all out.

Once you're done writing, allow yourself to sink into your bath. Hear your breath and feel your body relax. Visualize yourself as The Hermit, alone atop a mountain. What does the landscape around you look like? What do you hear? Simply observe and be, as you integrate with The Hermit's energy.

Look to The Hermit card for guidance and listen to his wisdom in your intuition. Sit with these feelings for a few minutes.

Using the flame of the candle, carefully light the paper on fire, releasing your worries to the Universe. Drop the paper into your cauldron or fireproof bowl to burn. Sprinkle a small amount of the cooled ashes in your bath to drain with the Epsom salts and lavender oil. Throw the rest of the cooled ashes in the bottom of a trash can, where it's dark, to quiet the noise they represent.

Repeat the spell as needed when the noise in your head becomes too loud.

JOURNAL QUESTIONS:

What is your relationship to solitude? Are you comfortable being alone? Why or why not? What areas of your life do you find solace and retreat in? Do you allow enough quiet time to hear the voices of your guides?

WHEEL OF FORTUNE: Change
Your Luck

Key words: Fortune, change, cycles

Welcome to Wheel! Of! Fortune! Our first contestant is you, witchy book-reading babe! In today's game, this wheel can bring you prizes, like new cars and vacations, and it can also bring loss, bad days, and difficult chapters of life. In tarot, the Wheel of Fortune is always spinning, in a constant state of change. Forever in motion, the Wheel of Fortune serves as a reminder that you can't control life, and things will flow more easily if you allow yourself to trust in the Universe that the wheel will come back around eventually. The Wheel of Fortune points out that, good or bad, nothing lasts forever.

 Wheel of Fortune

A Mirror Magick Spell for Good Luck

Timing: Waxing moon, Thursday

Sometimes it can feel like your spins keep landing on "bankrupt," leaving you in a seemingly never-ending unlucky streak, and that's when you can work your magick a bit to get the wheel to spin back in your favor. In this spell, you'll work with the ever-changing cyclical nature of the Wheel of Fortune to attract good luck.

What you need:

- Smoke for cleansing (herbal wand, incense, etc.)
- Small bowl
- 1 basil sprig
- Small mirror
- Sieve
- Wheel of Fortune tarot card
- 1 teaspoon ground allspice

This spell is to be cast over a period of seven days. Begin by cleansing all four corners of the room to remove old and stagnant energy, so your new luck can enter a space with a clean slate.

Set out a small bowl containing a basil sprig, an herb associated with luck and prosperity, as an offering to the Universe for helping to change your luck.

Place a small mirror flat on your work space and set a sieve on top of the mirror. The sieve works to filter out bad luck, while the mirror reflects back the good.

Place the Wheel of Fortune tarot card inside the sieve, in its reversed position–with the top facing away from you. Sprinkle the allspice, for attracting good luck, on top of the card.

Day one: Leave the mirror in this position for today.

Every day for the next six days, turn the mirror clockwise to your right. As you turn it, say,

Wheel of Fortune, as you turn,
Sift out my bad luck.
One rotation, once around,
Only good luck will be stuck.

By the last day, the mirror should be turned 180 degrees, so the Wheel of Fortune is facing you in its upright position.

You have now "spun" the Wheel of Fortune tarot card one full rotation, changing your luck.

JOURNAL QUESTIONS:

Your inner dialogue is often reflected back to you in the outside world: How can you change your inner voice to a more positive one? The Wheel of Fortune asks you to trust in the divine timing of the Universe: Where can you try to release a little control over things? How much of life do you believe is luck? How much do you believe you have influence over?

JUSTICE: Reveal the Truth

How often in your life have you thought, "If only they could see the *truth*!" Justice thinks that all the time, too. Justice is a pillar of fairness, truth, and accountability. A keeper of balance, Justice is wide-eyed, seeing all and ready to impart a ruling swiftly and firmly. This card reminds us, though, that Justice is a two-way street and a double-edged sword; it's not only about consequences, but also accountability.

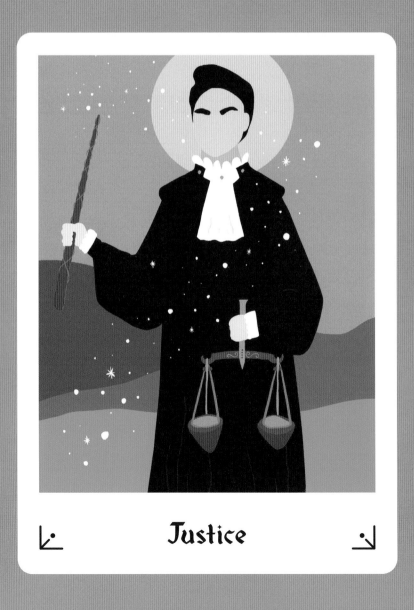

Justice

A Sun Water Spell for Truth

Timing: Waxing or full moon

It can be frustrating when others aren't able to see a truth so clear to you, and that's when working with the Justice card can be beneficial. Remain aware, though, that the truth does have consequences. In this spell, you'll work with the energy of the Justice card to reveal the truth.

What you need:

- Justice tarot card
- Sun water (below)
- Bowl
- Lighter or matchbook
- Sandalwood incense and holder

Sun Water

Sun water is pretty much what it sounds like . . . water that has been left in sunlight to absorb the energy of the sun! A powerful and potent way to work with the cosmic energy of the Sun in spellwork, sun water carries properties of illumination, clarity, strength, and healing.

To make sun water, take a clear glass cup, jar, or bowl of water and set it outside to charge in the sunlight for an hour or so before your spell. Ideally, sun water is left to charge all day, but in a pinch some sunlight is better than none! Collect your sun water and bring it inside. If you're unable to set it outside due to weather, set your water on a windowsill that gets direct sunlight.

Begin by focusing your intentions for the spell and what truth you're asking to be revealed. Set the Justice tarot card facedown on your work space, closing off Justice's eyes to the truth.

Pour the sun water into the bowl. The sun brings illumination to the truth. Visualize a beam of white light coming from the sun water, shooting upright, as strong and sturdy as the sword in Justice's hand.

Light your sandalwood incense, for awakening and clarity. Pass the smoke over the bowl nine times; nine is the number of Justice, further charging the sun water.

Dip two fingers into the charged sun water and close your eyes. Place your fingers at one side of your temple, dragging them over your closed eyes to the other temple. As you do, say,

Open my eyes, light of the sun,
May the truth be revealed and justice done.

If you are intending for the truth to be revealed to someone else, envision that person as you anoint your eyes with the charged sun water.

Open your eyes and turn the Justice card over, so that it's faceup, eyes able to see the truth.

Repeat as needed before conversations or events where you want the truth to be revealed.

JOURNAL QUESTIONS:

If others are unable to see your truth, what are possible reasons they may be unclear on the situation? If the truth is revealed and justice is served, how will you feel? Check in here to ensure your wish for the truth to be revealed is not ego driven. Is it possible that you've been keeping the truth from yourself out of fear of dealing with the fallout?

THE HANGED MAN: Surrender to the Universe

Key words: Surrender, pause, let go

The Hanged Man appears unassuming. He wears an expression of contentment, as he hangs from a tree covered in greenery. It's rather serene. The wisdom is one of the more difficult lessons: The Hanged Man asks you to sit in the space of unknowing—and make a cup of tea while you're there because you will need to get comfortable with being uncomfortable. The Hanged Man asks us to embrace stillness and surrender all expectations to the Universe. Stillness, surrender, pause, letting go . . . now, that's the trick.

The Hanged Man

A Gratitude and Grounding Spell for Surrender

Timing: Dark moon

As modern witches, many of us are uncomfortable with sitting in a place of pause. Doing, going, creating, moving–it all comes more naturally to us. Stillness feels foreign. In this spell, you'll work with The Hanged Man to surrender to the Universe. This spell is best performed outside to establish a connection to the Earth.

What you need:

- 2 pieces of paper
- Pen
- Small cauldron or fireproof bowl
- Lighter or matchbook
- Small rock
- String
- The Hanged Man tarot card

Find a quiet spot to sit outside. Spend a few minutes connecting with the Earth; visualize your body forming roots that go to the core of the Earth. You are a part of the Earth and the Universe, made from stardust

On one piece of paper, write what you're surrendering to the Universe: fears, expectations, anything you're ready to let go of. On the second paper, write what you're grateful for.

Place the paper containing what you're surrendering in a small cauldron and light it on fire, releasing it to the Universe. Visualize the weights being lifted from your body.

Fold the paper with what you're grateful for three times, each time folding toward yourself and turning it clockwise as you fold to draw its energy to you. Place a small rock inside the paper, and use the string to tie the paper and rock together, creating a weight. The weight of your gratitude far outweighs the ashes of what you're releasing. Scatter the cooled ashes into the wind to fully surrender to the Universe.

Lie on the ground in the position of The Hanged Man, holding your gratitude weight. Feel your connection to the Earth. Spend time in the stillness and acknowledge any feelings that come up. Surrender your whole being to the divine plans and timing of the Universe.

At home, set the gratitude weight on your altar on top of The Hanged Man card on a windowsill to charge in the light of the moon for the night, releasing any leftover fear.

The next day, bury your gratitude weight in a potted plant, releasing it to the Universe to continue to grow. As your plant grows with gratitude in its soil, it's a reminder that it's safe to surrender to the Universe, because it will always be there, helping you grow.

JOURNAL QUESTIONS:

Why does it feel uncomfortable to be still? What feelings come up? Why is surrender so hard? What are you worried may happen? How can you view things from a new perspective? What if you focused your energy on things working out?

DEATH: Say Goodbye to the Old You

Key words: Endings, transition, change

Although undoubtedly one of the more ominous cards in tarot, Death isn't a card of fear or pain. Death brings us endings, change, and transition: getting fired from your job only to find a more desirable one, breaking up with a partner and focusing on a better relationship with yourself, losing one thing to gain another. Death brings us the end of something, and in the midst of that, yes, things can get messy and difficult. However, Death can be a comforting card if you choose to view it as the Universe having your back; a chapter of your life is ending, so that another more aligned one can begin.

Death

A Burial Spell for Transformation

Timing: Full moon

When Death shows up, something has to change–and that change will likely require a new version of yourself. In this spell, you will work with the Death card to say goodbye to the old version of yourself so you can step into the next version of you as you move through endings and transition into a new chapter of life.

What you need:

- Death tarot card
- Paper and pen
- Something that represents the old you: a photo, business card, or anything meaningful to you
- Coffee grounds
- White rose petals

Begin your spell by meditating on the Death card. Enter the tarot card in your meditation: What version of yourself has died or is dying? What emotions come up for you surrounding your death? What does the armor-clad skeleton (immortal) version of you look like? What version of yourself will have evolved once the sun fully rises in the morning?

Write down the "old" version of yourself on your piece of paper. This represents the version of you that has died and that you are laying to rest.

Bury your paper outside, with the symbol of something that represents the old you and the previous chapter of your life. Once buried, sprinkle coffee grounds, representative of graveyard dirt, on the ground atop your buried paper. Sprinkle the white rose petals as an offering to your old self.

Spend a few minutes at your "grave" giving a proper burial to your old self as you thank the past version of you for all they have done. Feel through any emotions that come up. Revisit this spot when you need a reminder of how far you've come.

JOURNAL QUESTIONS:

What aspects of yourself or your old identity are no longer serving you? Why? What have you learned from the version of yourself that has "died"? What will be required of you as you transition into the next chapter? How will you grow, expand, and transform?

TEMPERANCE: Balance Your Energy

Key words: Balance, middle road, calm

In a society of extremes, calm and inner peace can be difficult to come by. Temperance teaches one of the more difficult lessons in tarot: finding the middle road, not allowing yourself to become carried away, and maintaining internal harmony as you walk through life. Maybe it feels like sprouting giant red wings à la the angel of Temperance and learning to fly would be easier than that . . . it's tricky! When your energy is out of balance, though, you can end up with that "off" feeling that you can't seem to shake. Try to relax and practice peace, rather than resisting every step of the way.

Temperance

An Elemental Spell to Cultivate Calm

Timing: Noon

Temperance asks you to come back to homeostasis and chill there for a little while. In this spell, you'll work with the calm, middle-of-the-road energy of Temperance to balance your energy.

What you need:

- Lighter or matchbook
- Yellow chime candle
- Temperance tarot card
- Paper and pen
- 2 cups
- Feather (any color)
- Flower (any flower)
- Bowl of water

Light your yellow candle, representative of the peace found at the end of the middle road in the Temperance card.

Place your hands on your heart and breathe in deeply three times, picturing a field of white light surrounding you that contracts and expands with every breath.

Keeping your hands at your heart, visualize yourself as the angel in the Temperance card, peaceful and calm. What has been throwing your energy off-balance lately? Picture these things on either side of the road you're standing on, not affecting you, as you stand balanced in the middle.

Place the Temperance tarot card at the top of your work space. On your paper, draw a middle path, symbolizing the one in the card. Place one cup on each side of your path, and your candle at the end.

Place your feather next to the left cup, representing flighty airy energy, and the flower next to the right cup, representing grounded earthy energy.

Pour all of the water into one of the cups–whichever cup you feel your energy is heavier in at the moment, Air or Earth. As you pour, visualize all that is throwing your energy off-kilter flowing out of your body and into the water. Extinguish your candle.

On the second day, light your candle and transfer all the water to the other cup. Again, visualizing your energy moving with the water. Extinguish the candle.

On the third day, light your candle and pour half of the water into the other cup, so each cup is half full and balanced. The water in the cups symbolizes your balanced energy. Extinguish your candle.

Leave the cups in their balanced state for four more days, one week total, to complete the spell. Repeat the three-day balancing once more during that week, if needed.

JOURNAL QUESTIONS:

What does the middle road look like for you? What emotions do you feel (and not feel) there? What does alignment feel like in your physical body? What self-care can you practice to feel more calm and at peace?

THE DEVIL: Banish Self-Sabotage

In the Rider-Waite-Smith tarot, The Devil is portrayed as the deity Baphomet. Less a card of eternal damnation in hell, The Devil is more a card of restriction and limitation, as evidenced by the couple enslaved by The Devil's chains. The Devil comes up when you've been playing small, grappling with issues such as attachment or self-sabotage . . . anything that keeps you from being and believing in your highest, most magickal self. The Devil asks you to look inward and find the places you've been allowing limitations to dictate your life, and conversely, how you can loosen those chains around your neck.

The Devil

A Banishing Oil Candle Spell for Self-Sabotage

Timing: Waning moon, Saturday

It can feel good temporarily to give in to stories about why you're holding yourself back, but it only prolongs the pain that will inevitably come once you face the truth. In this spell, you'll work with The Devil tarot card to banish self-sabotage so you can take on the world (or at least finally tackle your to-do list).

What you need:

- Black chime candle
- String, about 24 inches (61 cm) long
- The Devil tarot card
- Toothpick or safety pin
- Glass bottle or jar
- Olive oil
- Rosemary (diluted essential oil or dried herb)
- Lemon peel
- Peppercorns
- Garlic clove
- Lighter or matchbook
- Scissors
- Small cauldron or fireproof bowl

Begin by holding the black candle and meditating or thinking about ways you self-sabotage. How does self-sabotage show up for you? What does it keep you from accomplishing? As you think about these things, tie the string (loosely!) around your neck, representing the hold that self-sabotage has over you.

Working with The Devil tarot card, visualize yourself in the card, chains of self-sabotage around your neck. Hold this visual in your mind as you carve your candle with the toothpick. What you carve can be a word that describes the way self-sabotage shows up, such as "procrastination," the word "self-sabotage" itself, or whatever feels right for you. Remember, this is a banishing spell, so what you carve should represent what you want to banish.

Create a banishing oil in your glass bottle or jar by filling it with olive oil as your carrier oil. Add a bit of rosemary for banishing and calling in transformation, lemon peel for cleansing and purification, peppercorns to banish negative thoughts, and a garlic clove for protection. There are no set amounts for these ingredients; let your intuition lead you as to how much of each to add.

Anoint your candle with your banishing oil by rubbing oil onto your fingers and then rubbing the oil from the top of the candle, near the wick, to the bottom.

Light your candle and visualize the chains of self-sabotage loosening around your neck, until you're free from them.

When you feel ready, cut the string from around your neck, and burn it in a small cauldron or fireproof bowl, freeing yourself from the chains of self-sabotage. Extinguish your candle and throw the cooled ashes of your chain away in the trash, where they belong!

JOURNAL QUESTIONS:

What false stories are you telling yourself that allow the self-sabotage cycle to continue? What part of your identity is attached to these stories? What could your life look like if you stopped sabotaging your greatness?

THE TOWER: Embrace Change During Chaotic Times

Key words: Endings, transition, change

The Tower heralds in times of chaos, change, and upheaval. Sometimes in life, your tower gets destroyed (although hopefully not in the literal hit-by-lightning manner of the Rider-Waite-Smith depiction). Things feel like they're crumbling, and the foundation on which you've built your relationship, job, or even life feels as if it's slipping away beneath your feet as you struggle to find new solid ground. The thing is, when it's destroyed, it leaves a space for a new tower, one even stronger and more aligned than the one before it.

The Tower

A Crystal and Candles Spell for Change

Timing: Full moon or sunset

In the midst of your Tower season, it can be difficult to see the light at the end of the tunnel that seems to collapse in on you. In this spell, you'll work with The Tower to embrace change during chaotic times.

What you need:

- Lighter or matchbook
- 3 black chime candles
- Lepidolite crystal
- White string or thread
- The Tower tarot card
- Black pen
- Paper
- Small cauldron or fireproof bowl

Light three black candles and place them in a triangle shape on your altar. The triangle symbolizes strength in the darkness of the black chaos of The Tower card. Place your lepidolite crystal, with calming properties, and white string, symbolizing hope, in the center of the candle triangle.

Sit with The Tower card and meditate on or visualize you and your circumstance in The Tower. What do you feel is falling apart around you? What was the lightning-strike catalyst that set this situation in motion? See if you can remove yourself from the situation and view it from an outside perspective: Separate yourself from the chaos and fear, as an observer, knowing the emotions are there, but not allowing them to swallow or define you.

Write down your fears in black ink on paper. Light three corners of the paper on fire, one corner from each candle, and place it in your cauldron to burn, releasing your fears into the Universe. As it burns, say aloud,

In the dark the tower falls
Hope and light, hear my call.
As I walk through the dust, I welcome change,
The cards fall, things rearrange.
With strength,
With confidence,
With power,
I do not fear the destruction of The Tower.

As the candles are burning, hold your lepidolite and white string and focus on what is being rebuilt. How has this circumstance given you the opportunity to move forward in an even more aligned way? What good can you find?

Extinguish your candles. Sleep with the lepidolite under your pillow to elicit calm during the night when minds run wild with worry and tie the white string around your wrist as a reminder of the good that is to come through your Tower moment. When it falls off, you will have moved on to the next chapter of your life.

JOURNAL QUESTIONS:

During a time that feels chaotic and out of your control, what is one small thing you can do for yourself to help bring calm? How is the Universe working for you right now? How can you rebuild your tower even stronger?

THE STAR: Find Your Purpose

The Star brings rebirth, hope, and purpose. It's that sparkly, warm, golden glow feeling, when things are aligning and you're filled with optimism and intention as you move forward after a period of darkness. The figure in The Star stands naked in her authenticity, assured, grounded, and trusting in her intuition to lead her where she is destined to be.

The Star

A Water Scrying Spell to Find Your Purpose

Timing: Waxing moon

As modern witches, it can be tricky to get clear on your purpose here on this wild planet. If questions like, "What am I supposed to do with my life?" or, "How am I meant to serve others?" plague you at night, this spell is for you! In this spell, you'll work with The Star to find your purpose.

What you need:

- Chamomile tea
- Spoon
- Spirit quartz crystal
- Black bowl filled with water
- Amethyst crystal
- The Star tarot card

Make a cup of chamomile tea, and with your spoon, stir clockwise three times as you think of your intentions for this spell. Sip your chamomile tea, for intuition and calm, throughout the spell.

Pick up your spirit quartz and tap it gently on the North, South, East, and West sides of the bowl, and then stir the water with it three times clockwise as you say aloud,

Stir up my intuition, water wise,
Show me the wisdom of The Star,
Let me see it with my eyes.

Repeat this step with the amethyst.

Sit cross-legged on the floor, in front of your bowl of water. Holding the spirit quartz, for spiritual connection, in one hand and the amethyst, for intuition, in the other, close your eyes.

Meditate on or visualize yourself walking through the lush field pictured in The Star. As you continue walking, you hear the gentle babble of a brook, leading to a lake. You come across a goddess-like figure standing half in, half out of the lake. You stop and ask her, "What is my purpose?" What does she say?

Open your eyes and use your bowl of water for water scrying—to scry means to look at an object to find a message. Drop the spirit quartz into the water and study the ripples. What do you see in the water? What shapes or visions appear? What does your intuition tell you? Repeat with the amethyst.

Know that this spell will likely take time, and that the answer may not appear right away. Don't get discouraged if an answer does not immediately appear.

To continue the spell, you may choose to keep your water bowl on your altar and anoint your third eye with the spell water before you go to sleep. Sleep with The Star card under your pillow. Pay close attention to your dreams for messages from your guides.

JOURNAL QUESTIONS:

What did you want to do or be when you were a child? What natural gifts or talents do you have? What do others come to you for help with? What signs show up that may be pointing your way?

THE MOON: Clear Confusion Around a Decision

Key words: Illusion, fear, confusion

The Moon in tarot gives off an almost fairy-take-like energy. Placing yourself within the context of this card would likely feel as if walking through a hazy dream, where a strange fog has seeped into the surroundings and things feel just slightly . . . off. It's the feeling you get when you wake up from an unsettling dream and are in that blurry state between awake and asleep. A card of illusion, fear, and confusion, The Moon card often appears when you're not quite clear on something, and feelings of confusion are clouding your vision.

The Moon

A Charm Spell for Clarity

Timing: Waxing or full moon

The Moon card asks you to trust your intuition to find the truth in the darkness, to sift through the clouds of illusion and get clarity. In this spell, you'll work with the energy of The Moon to clear confusion around a decision.

What you need:

- Lavender tea
- Peppermint essential oil (diluted)
- Lighter or matchbook
- Silver chime candle
- Thumbtack or pushpin
- The Moon tarot card

Begin by making a cup of lavender tea, to promote calm. While your tea is steeping, rub a drop of peppermint essential oil on your temples and third eye, for clarity.

Take your tools into a room and light a silver chime candle, for connection to your intuition. Set the thumbtack, representing sharpness of mind, on top of The Moon tarot card, representing confusion, and turn off the lights. The darkness in the room reflects the darkness in the night of The Moon card.

Focus on your intention and what you're feeling confused about, and the decision you're seeking clarity on. Shine the light of the silver chime candle, casting the light of your intuition onto the thumbtack and The Moon card, and say,

Sharp as a tack, confusion be gone,
I will have clarity on this decision by dawn.

Sip your lavender tea while the silver chime candle burns. You can take this time to journal thoughts or feelings that are surfacing. What does your intuition tell you? Notice any signs that come during the spell and throughout the rest of the day or night.

That night, sleep with the thumbtack under your bed (not your pillow!). Confusion will be lessened, and you'll be clear on your decision when you wake up. If you're not super clear when you wake up, keep the thumbtack under your bed until you wake up with the answer.

JOURNAL QUESTIONS:

Have your dreams brought any clarity or messages regarding the situation? Is fear playing a role in the confusion you're experiencing? When you think about this decision, what do you feel in your physical body? What is your intuition telling you through this?

THE SUN: INCREASE SELF-CONFIDENCE

Key words: Happiness, confidence, joy

The Sun is a card of happiness, confidence, and joy–those feelings you get on a warm spring day, when you're outside surrounded by flowers, the sun kisses your cheek, and all feels right with the world. The Sun reminds you of the good in life, and that childlike joy is always available to you. If things aren't going so great now, hold the faith that they will be well again soon. The Sun card is also a source of power and confidence–after all, our sun is one of the key elements that nurtures life on Earth!

The Sun

A Mirror Magick Spell for Confidence

Timing: Sunday

Being filled with the energy of The Sun means being unapologetically you and feeling confident AF in who you are and what you do. On days when you're feeling less sunshine and rainbows, this spell will help increase your self-confidence with the wisdom of The Sun so you can get back to and remember your sparkly self.

What you need:

- A badass babe music playlist
- Clothing that makes you feel beautiful
- Yellow flowers
- Full-length mirror
- The Sun tarot card
- Pen
- Tape

Put on an upbeat playlist that inspires confidence, and adorn yourself in clothing, makeup, perfume, etc., that makes you feel beautiful and powerful. You can also do this spell nude if you choose.

Create a circle of yellow flowers in front of your mirror with enough space for you in the middle, and sit in the circle of flowers, with The Sun card in front of you. Yellow flowers inspire beauty, happiness, and confidence; here, they represent the yellow flowers seen in The Sun card, and the circle of yellow symbolizes the sun itself.

Close your eyes and visualize a bright yellow light surrounding your circle, glowing warm and expanding outward with each breath you take.

Open your eyes, and truly see yourself for the beautiful and confident witch that you are. What do you like about your physical appearance? What are good qualities that you possess? Write down these things on The Sun card. You can print an image of The Sun card and use that if you choose not to use the card from your deck, or a piece of yellow paper will work, too.

Choose one flower and pluck the petals from it. Scatter the petals over The Sun card and say aloud,

Yellow and bright, radiant as the sun,
Confidence and self-love, not easily won.
I call upon my inner knowing to remind me,
Card, words, and mirror, sealed with petals three.

Tape The Sun card and three yellow flower petals to the back of your mirror so that when you look in it, the things you love and admire about yourself that make you feel confident will be reflected back to you.

Dry the rest of the flowers and use them as ingredients in spells for self-love, confidence, and happiness.

JOURNAL QUESTIONS:

What simple acts bring you joy? How can you incorporate more of those into your every day? Where do you need more of The Sun's happy light? What is your source of inner power?

JUDGMENT: Overcome Self-Doubt

Key words: Reflection, inner calling, self-evaluation

You know that saying "You're your own worst critic"? Enter: the Judgment card! Judgment is a card of reflection and listening to that inner voice that's calling you to level up. Pulling Judgment often means that an awakening is near or, at the very least, you'll be faced with making a big decision soon. The thing about all of this is . . . we tend not to be great listeners. Judgment strides grandly into the room, blowing its trumpet in your face, urging you, "Wake up! Wake up!" And suddenly, faced with such gravity and understanding that leveling up will require you to grow and challenge yourself . . . self doubt creeps in.

Judgment

A Banishing Spell for Self-Doubt

Timing: Full moon or Saturday

Allowing past mistakes to define you ultimately holds you back from your cosmic calling. In this spell, you'll work with the Judgment card to overcome self-doubt so that you can answer Judgment's call confidently.

What you need:

- Judgment tarot card
- 2 small strips of paper
- Pen
- Bell

Begin your spell by meditating for two minutes on the Judgment card and what you're doubting yourself about. What is holding you back from believing in yourself? What could you accomplish if you overcame your self-doubt?

On your two small strips of paper, write "self-doubt" on one and "judgment" on the other. Stand in the middle of the room, holding the papers in one hand and the bell in the other. The bell represents the trumpet on the Judgment card, and is also a tool commonly used in banishing.

Ring your bell once to banish self-doubt and say,

Judgment and self-doubt no more,
Vanish as I walk through the door.
I overcome you with every step I take,
Belief in myself, now unable to shake.

Turn toward each corner of the room, ring your bell three times, and say, *Self-doubt, you are no longer welcome here.*

Take the two strips of paper and place one in the bottom of each shoe. Take a walk, preferably up a hill, and visualize your self-doubt getting smaller with each step you take, squashing it until it disappears. When you arrive back home, tear up the papers and throw them away to rid yourself of doubt.

JOURNAL QUESTIONS:

What is your purpose in life? How has self-doubt held you back from it? What emotions come up when you think of fulfilling your calling? Where does your lack of faith in yourself come from? What evidence do you have that you *are* enough to pursue your purpose?

THE WORLD: Manifest Success

Key words: Success, celebration, accomplishment

The last card in the major arcana, The World encompasses integration of the lessons learned throughout the successful completion of a cycle. The World often comes up in readings when you've just finished a big project or are closing out a chapter of your life. The hard work you've been putting in has paid off, and you're feeling grateful and accomplished. But what if you're not quite there yet? The World is a great card to work with when you're manifesting the success of something. The key to manifesting is tapping into the energy of already having it.

The World

A Letter Writing Spell for Success

Timing: New moon or Thursday

Learn to act as if you've already succeeded! In this spell, you'll tap into the celebratory and accomplished energy of The World to manifest success.

What you need:

- "Congratulations" card
- Pen
- Dried bay leaf
- $21
- Frankincense oil (diluted)
- The World tarot card

Purchase a "Congratulations" card that relates to what you're manifesting (e.g., a new house, new job, wedding card for a relationship, etc.).

Once home, write a congratulations note to yourself inside the card, acting as if you've already succeeded in your manifestation. Be detailed, including how you feel and specifics about your manifestation.

Sign your name on the bay leaf, for success, and place it inside the card.

Add the $21 to the card as a gift to yourself. Twenty-one is the number of The World in the major arcana. (Who doesn't love cards that come with money?!)

Seal the envelope, closing the fold toward your body to draw its energy to you, and write your name and address on the outside. Place a drop of frankincense oil, for success, on your fingertip, and draw a circle with the oil around your name, circling you in success.

Hold the envelope to your heart and say,

Success I claim, in written name.
In timing divine, my manifestations align.

Place the card on your altar on top of The World card while you work toward your manifestation. Once you have succeeded in your manifestation, open the card, read your note to yourself, and use the $21 to buy yourself a little congratulatory gift. You deserve it!

JOURNAL QUESTIONS:

As you're manifesting the completion of a chapter, how have you changed since the beginning of this cycle? Allow yourself to reflect on your success; what are you proud of? What new beginning will this manifestation allow you to start?

The Minor Arcana

T HE MINOR ARCANA ARE CARDS
THAT RELATE TO DAY-TO-DAY
HAPPENINGS; THE SPELLS IN THIS
SECTION COVER PRACTICAL OR
EVERYDAY SITUATIONS.

Two of Cups

Four of Cups

Five of Cups

Seven of Cups

Nine of Cups

Three of Wands

Two of Swords

Four of Pentacles

Kni

King of Cups

Ace of Wands

Four of Wands

Eight of Swords

Eight of Wands

Page of Wands

Knight of Wands

Queen of Wands

Ace

ACE OF CUPS: Attract New Love

Key words: Opportunity, love, new beginnings

If you've been pulling the Ace of Cups often recently, the gods and goddesses are on your side, babe! The Ace of Cups is equivalent to the moment a main character in a teen movie finally realizes their potential, gets a slammin' makeover, and struts into school like they own the place; suddenly opportunities open up to them and they've got the world at their fingertips. The Ace of Cups represents new opportunity, new beginnings, and the potential for your cup to overflow with love and creativity.

Ace of Cups

A Love Letter Spell

Timing: New moon or Friday

When focusing on manifesting new love, the Ace of Cups is an ideal card to work with, because it signifies being receptive to new energies and vibrating on an excited and limitless frequency. In this spell, you'll work with the Ace of Cups to attract a new love into your life.

What you need:

- Romantic music
- Optional: lighter or matchbook
- Optional: pink or red candles
- Rosewater (can use a drop of rose essential oil in water), enough to fill the gold cup
- Gold cup
- ¼ cup (9 g) dried rose petals
- Spoon
- Red pen
- Paper
- Ace of Cups tarot card
- 4 small magnets

Begin by putting on romantic music and focusing on your intention for this spell. You may choose to light pink or red candles to further set the mood. Pink and red are colors often used in love spells because of their associations with romantic love and passion.

Add your rosewater, for love, to your gold cup, representing the cup seen in the Ace of Cups. Sprinkle in rose petals for attraction and desire. With your spoon, stir the rosewater three times clockwise, while focusing on the love that you're drawing into your life with this spell.

Dip your finger into the cup and anoint your heart space with the love potion. Do this by picturing your heart activating and opening, its energy receptive and ready for new love, as you rub the love potion over your heart.

Spend two to three minutes visualizing the love you're manifesting. What do they look like? How do they make you feel? What do the two of you do together? Write everything down with your red pen, associated with the goddess Venus, on your paper. Be specific and write in the present tense, as if this person is already in your life.

Dip a finger into the love potion and seal your love letter with a heart. Place your love letter on your altar with the Ace of Cups card on top of it, and four magnets, one on each side, to attract love to you. Use the rest of your love potion in love spells or on yourself before dates.

JOURNAL QUESTIONS:

What is your heart asking for? Where do you close yourself off to opportunity? When was a time when you felt truly loved?

TWO OF CUPS: Strengthen Your Relationship

Key words: Partnership, attraction, unity

The Two of Cups centers on partnership, attraction, and love. It is that initial spark and attraction felt when you meet someone new, when things are just beginning and there's unlimited potential. The Two of Cups is about two people choosing to work together and build their relationship. If you've been in a long-term relationship, things can become mundane and routine, and a focus on building your relationship can get put on the back burner in favor of the day-to-day things. You can forget that working together is key to keeping your relationship strong and maintaining the butterflies felt in the beginning.

Two of Cups

A Bond-Strengthening Spell

Timing: Friday, Sunday, or the waxing moon

Sometimes that initial Two of Cups spark can get a bit forgotten as you move onto bigger life choices. In this spell, you'll work with the Two of Cups to strengthen your relationship.

What you need:

- Ring (can be costume jewelry, it's more about the symbolism)
- Strand of your hair
- Strand of your partner's hair
- 2 pieces of red ribbon, about 8 to 10 inches (20 to 26 cm) long
- Red envelope
- Two of Cups tarot card

Begin by holding the ring to your heart space. Visualize the bond you and your partner have; the ring represents your relationship.

Next, take the strand of your hair and one piece of the red ribbon. Tie them together to the ring. Do the same with your partner's hair and the second ribbon. The strands of hair act as a taglock, or an item that connects a specific person to your spell.

You should now have two segments, one representing you and one representing your partner. Take both segments, and tie them into one knot, strengthening your bond. Say aloud,

In one knot is found two,
may the strength of our bond be true.
Love encircled in endless ring,
May this spell, strength in our relationship bring.

Place the ring in a red envelope, along with the Two of Cups tarot card, and seal it closed, sealing the strength in your relationship.

Place the envelope in a place with sunlight to charge it with the sun's strength. Store the spell under your mattress to strengthen your relationship.

JOURNAL QUESTIONS:

How do you express your feelings in your relationship? How can you show up more thoughtfully for your relationship? What defines a "strong relationship" to you?

THREE OF CUPS:
Make New Friends

Key words: Friendship, community, social gatherings

The Three of Cups shows three friends coming together dancing and celebrating. Like Carrie, Samantha, Charlotte, and Miranda on *Sex and the City,* these pals are close-knit and having a good time, drinks in hand. A card of overall happiness and good vibes, the Three of Cups is definitely the party card of the minor arcana. As adults, though, it's generally agreed upon that forming new friendships can be difficult. In classic Carrie Bradshaw fashion, I couldn't help but wonder, how can you work with the Three of Cups to assist in making new friends?

Three of Cups

A *Cupcake Magick Spell*

Timing: Any day, morning, or afternoon

Whether it's the result of moving, changing jobs, or simply drifting away from high school and college relationships, the camaraderie of the Three of Cups seems harder and harder to come by. In this spell, you'll work with the Three of Cups to make new friends.

What you need:

- Cupcake recipe and ingredients, including icing
- Paper and pen
- Three of Cups tarot card

Note: Have one aspect of the recipe include lavender, strawberry, allspice, or clove, as they have correspondences to friendship.

Begin by making your cupcakes. As you mix the ingredients, picture yourself with your new friends, talking, laughing, and having fun. Stir your intentions into the cupcake batter by focusing on this visualization and stirring the batter clockwise three times before you pour it into the pan.

While your cupcakes are baking, write a sigil for friendship (see page 18) on the paper. While creating your sigil, study the Three of Cups tarot card. Focus on the qualities you're looking for in future friends, and the qualities you bring to the table as a good friend.

Once your cupcakes are cooled, draw the sigil in the icing of each cupcake, sweetening your intention by creating it in sugar. How you incorporate the sigil is up to you: You can ice the entire cupcake and discreetly draw it in with a toothpick, or include the sigil as a decorative element.

As you draw the sigil in the icing, say aloud,

Sweetened will new connections be,
Relationships come easily,
New friends, new friends, I call to me,
As in the card with cups of three.

Take your cupcakes to share at a social event or invite prospective friends over for cupcakes and tea to complete the spell.

JOURNAL QUESTIONS:

What qualities are important to you in a friendship? How do you show up for others in a friendship? What can you do to add more celebration into your life and better celebrate the little things?

FOUR OF CUPS: Renew Inspiration

Key words: Boredom, discontentment, disconnection

If you feel "bleh" about things and generally unmotivated (and maybe a little moody), you've already got that Four of Cups energy down pat! In the Rider-Waite-Smith illustration, the Four of Cups features a discontented man sitting cross-legged under a tree, bored with life and unimpressed with what's being offered. We tend to find ourselves embodying this energy when the inspiration tank is low and we're running out of motivation to move forward. Nothing seems quite as exciting and shiny as it did initially, and you may ask, "What's the point?"

 Four of Cups

A Spell to Invoke Inspiration

Timing: Wednesday or any day in the morning

Time to bust out of that rut, babe! In this spell, you'll work with the Four of Cups to renew your inspiration and get creative again.

What you need:

- Page of inspiration (see Note)
- 1 teaspoon grated fresh ginger
- 1 teaspoon cayenne pepper
- 1 teaspoon coffee grounds or whole beans
- Sprinkle of biodegradable gold glitter
- Four of Cups tarot card
- Small amethyst crystal
- 4 orange chime candles and holders
- Lighter or matchbook
- Citrus tea

Note: For inspiration, choose a document representative of what you're seeking. For example, a page of a book for writer's block, a printed picture of a work of art you admire for artistic inspiration, a grocery receipt or printed recipe for cooking inspiration. Get creative!

Place your document in the middle of your work space. Sprinkle the grated ginger over the document for a zingy burst of energy, cayenne for a boost of heat and motivation, coffee for a jolt of energy and alertness, and biodegradable gold glitter to reflect positivity.

Place the Four of Cups in its reversed position, denoting happiness and clarity in the center, with an amethyst crystal on top, to facilitate insight and vision.

Place the four orange candles, representing the four cups in the Four of Cups, at each corner of your document. The color orange is associated with energy and motivation. Light your candles, surrounding your subject with light, motivation, and inspiration.

Hold both hands above the flames and say,

Inspiration I call,
I am out of this rut, once and for all.
With golden vision now I see
the picture clearly in front of me.

Get to work and begin your project with renewed motivation as the candles burn.

Make a cup of citrus tea to sip on while you work; citrus helps you feel awake and energized.

JOURNAL QUESTIONS:

What makes you feel discontent or lacking in motivation? Do you need to take a break to reset? For how long? What is one thing you can do to keep yourself focused on the goal?

FIVE OF CUPS: Cope with Grief

Key words: Sadness, loss, regret

A somber card of loss and regret, the Five of Cups suggests being focused on the negative, rather than the positive that's still present in your life. During a Five of Cups season of life, you'll likely find yourself in the throes of grief or sorrow; it's okay to linger here for a minute. No service is done by trying to rush the grieving process. However, don't allow yourself to forget the wonderful things and people still in your life.

Five of Cups

A Ritual for Grief

Timing: Full moon

While the figure in the Five of Cups has allowed themselves to become lost and swallowed in grief, you don't have to. In this spell, you'll work with the Five of Cups in a grief ritual, to feel through grief, while leaning into the positives surrounding you.

What you need:

- Cup
- ½ cup (112 g) Epsom salts
- 1 tablespoon (4 g) dried thyme
- 1 tablespoon (3 g) dried rosemary
- Handful of jasmine petals
- Five of Cups tarot card

In your cup, combine the Epsom salts for healing, thyme for grief, rosemary for comfort and the preservation of memories, and jasmine petals for loss and mix together. Hold the cup to your heart space and focus on your grief. Visualize the energy flowing from your body into the contents of the cup.

Next, pour the contents on top of the Five of Cups card. This represents the overturned cups in the Five of Cups. Using the salt mixture, form a word or symbol on top of the Five of Cups card from the "spilled grief," such as a heart, the word "love," or someone's name. This symbolizes the upright cups, the positive and good still present in your life. You may find a meditative quality as you form the salt into symbols or words. Take your time carefully arranging the crystals of salt and allow yourself to get lost in the practice.

Leave your salt creation on your work space as you work through grief as a reminder of the positives still in your life, or scoop it back into the cup and pour it into a hot bath that evening to soak in restoration and healing.

JOURNAL QUESTIONS:

When was the last time you dealt with major heartbreak or sadness? How did you cope then? What upright cups are still present in your life? Can forgiveness of someone else, or yourself, aid in this grieving process?

SIX OF CUPS: Heal Your Inner Child

Key words: Innocence, joy, memories

You know the saying: "Two things are certain in life: death and taxes." Well, they're forgetting a third . . . childhood trauma. Eek. I know, right? We've all got wounds and trauma from our childhood that continue to make themselves known into adulthood. In tarot, the Six of Cups guides you back to your childhood and aids you in reminiscing on happier times. Stepping into the space of your inner child allows you to revisit that energy and address wounds and traumas to work toward healing.

Six of Cups

A Spell to Reflect on and Heal Your Inner Child

Timing: Sunday

In this spell, you'll work with the Six of Cups to begin to heal your inner child. I encourage you to really step into the energy of your inner child by putting on some of your favorite childhood music or eating a nostalgic snack, to connect with your inner child before beginning this spell.

What you need:

- Photo of yourself as a child
- 6 pieces of paper
- Paper and pen
- Cup
- Fresh flower with white petals
- Rose quartz crystal
- Six of Cups tarot card

Begin by holding and focusing on the photo of yourself as a child. Close your eyes and take yourself back to then: What does your inner child look like? What are they wearing? What is their posture like?

Approach your inner child as your adult self now. Ask them how they're feeling and what they need. Listen.

On each of the six pieces of paper, representing the six cups in the Six of Cups, write down one way you will care for your inner child. These can be affirmations or playful activities to incorporate into your life, such as painting or dancing. They can be a resolution to begin therapy or shadow work. Note whatever your inner child is asking for.

Place the six pieces of paper in the cup and sprinkle the white flower petals, representing innocence, over them. As you do, say,

Inner child, I hear you,
Now begins our breakthrough.
I tend to your needs, as they are my own,
From innocence to now grown.

Place the rose quartz on top of the flower petals to seal the spell with unconditional love.

Pick one piece of paper and commit to working through what you promised your inner child.

Leave the cup and Six of Cups tarot card on a windowsill in the moonlight to soak in the nurturing energy of the moon as you work through healing your inner child.

JOURNAL QUESTIONS:

What brought you joy as a child? What did you want to do or be when you grew up? How can you incorporate more childlike joy into your life? What wounds from childhood are making themselves present now?

SEVEN OF CUPS: Break Free from Analysis Paralysis

Key words: Choices, indecision, hesitation

Chasing your dreams is never easy, and sometimes the hardest part is just taking that first step. In the Seven of Cups, you're presented with seven options: How do you decide which to choose? How often have you had a great idea that's died as just that—a great idea—because you suddenly became overwhelmed with analysis paralysis and couldn't figure out where to start? Like the figure in the Seven of Cups, you found yourself in a permanent place of pondering and overthinking, rather than trusting your instincts to grab a cup and start making moves.

 Seven of Cups

A Pendulum Spell for Guidance

Timing: Saturday

The Seven of Cups asks you to listen to your intuition and act, lest you find yourself stuck in dreamland, with your dreams forever out of reach. In this spell, you'll work with the Seven of Cups to break free from analysis paralysis and make a move.

What you need:

- Peppermint essential oil (diluted)
- Paper and pen
- Seven of Cups tarot card
- Lighter or matchbook
- Sandalwood incense and holder
- Pendulum

Sitting in a quiet space, dab the peppermint essential oil, for clear thinking, on your forehead, heart, palms of your hands, and bottoms of your feet.

Take two to three minutes and think through what you are overanalyzing. On the piece of paper, write down all the things you have to do but are unsure of where to begin. Rather than a list format, write each one down in a circle placed randomly on the paper, similar to the way the cups are scattered in the Seven of Cups card.

Light the sandalwood incense for clarity and hold it in front of the paper, so the smoke covers your list. Blow away the smoke to blow away the clouds of confusion.

Set the incense in its holder and take out your pendulum. Hold it over the paper and ask your guides, higher self, or the Universe to guide you in where to act and make your first move. The action in the circle that the pendulum guides you to is where to start.

JOURNAL QUESTIONS:

Is fear playing a part in the overwhelm you're experiencing? What are potential consequences of making (what you perceive to be) the wrong move? If you remain in this state of analysis paralysis for the next week, month, or year, where will that get you?

EIGHT OF CUPS: Cut Emotional Ties

Key words: Walking away, withdrawal, leaving behind

Walking away from things is tough . . . it's even harder to walk away from relationships that you've put time and effort into. Maybe you're still refreshing your ex's social media daily to keep tabs on them or can't help but respond to your toxic friend when they text. Whatever the case, the Eight of Cups suggests that it's time to pack it up and cut those emotional ties for good, babe. Cutting the tie may leave you feeling sad temporarily, but in the end will grant you the freedom to spend your energy on something more fulfilling.

Eight of Cups

A Cord-Cutting Spell

Timing: Full moon or Monday

Although you've spent time and effort cultivating this relationship, in the end, it's still left you feeling empty or lacking, and it's got to go. In this spell, you'll work with the Eight of Cups to cut emotional ties.

What you need:

- Body of water (river, lake, ocean, etc.) to perform spell at
- Black string or cord (several feet long)
- Scissors
- Small cauldron or fireproof bowl
- Lighter or matchbook
- Eight of Cups tarot card

Gather your spell tools and sit cross-legged at the water's edge. Hold the black cord in your open palms and picture the person you want to cut emotional ties with. Think of your relationship and how it's holding you back as you hold the cord and charge it with the emotional tie between you and the other person.

Still sitting cross-legged, tie your feet together with the cord; the binds of the emotional tie are now physical. Move your legs and feet a little and feel the resistance of the cord, the way it's restraining you. Sit with any emotions that arise.

When you feel ready, cut yourself free of the cord with scissors, and say aloud,

Black cords that tie me down,
I leave you here now on the ground.
With this I cut our emotional tie,
The bridge is burned, forever goodbye.

Place the cut cord in your cauldron and light it on fire. As the cord burns, visualize the emotional tie between you and the other person burning, and a shield of white light surrounding your energetic field, unwelcoming of their energy ever again.

Scatter the cooled ashes of the cord into the water to carry away your tie for good. Take a walk along the water's edge, holding the Eight of Cups card as you mirror its image, and feel the freedom as you can now move toward a more aligned path.

Keep the Eight of Cups card on your altar as a reminder that you have cut ties and walked away.

JOURNAL QUESTIONS:

Why have you been holding on to this relationship? What emotions come up as you leave this chapter behind? In what ways will your growth expand? Where will you go next?

NINE OF CUPS: Make Your Wish Come True

Key words: Wish come true, success, contentment

Often called the "wish card" or the "dreams come true card," the Nine of Cups represents that content feeling of satisfaction that washes over you once your dream has come true. It's always been in human nature to seek magick ways to fulfill wishes, from blowing out candles on your birthday cake to blowing on a dandelion as a child. It makes sense that we have the equivalent card in tarot. Don't forget to focus on the things in your life you already have and are grateful for, as gratitude tends to speed up the wish fulfillment process!

Nine of Cups

A Coin Wishing Spell

Timing: New moon

Pulling this card signifies that the Universe is conspiring in your favor to grant your wish, or that it's close to manifesting. In this spell, you'll work with the Nine of Cups to make your wish come true.

What you need:

- Bowl filled with water
- Blue lace agate crystal
- 9 pennies
- Nine of Cups tarot card
- Bell
- Gold pouch

Set down the bowl filled with water and sit cross-legged in front of it. Place the blue lace agate, for manifestation, at the bottom of the bowl.

Hold the nine pennies in your right hand and the Nine of Cups card in your left as you visualize your wish coming true. Toss each penny, one by one, into the bowl, as if tossing coins into a wishing well or fountain. As you toss each penny, say: *My wish comes true, and so it is* and ring the bell.

Leave the spell bowl in the moonlight to charge for nine nights. After nine nights, remove the pennies and blue lace agate and place them in the gold pouch, along with the Nine of Cups card.

Use the wish water to water a plant, to facilitate the growth of your wish. Keep the pouch with you in your wallet or bag until your wish has come true. Once it has, leave the pennies on your altar as an offering to the Universe to thank it for granting your wish.

JOURNAL QUESTIONS:

What do you want most in the world? How can you take a step toward getting that or making it happen? How will you feel once your wish has come true? Will you feel fulfilled?

TEN OF CUPS: Bring Peace to Your Home

Key words: Peaceful home, domestic harmony, happy family

The Ten of Cups portrays a happy and blessed family, picture perfect. It's pretty clear off the bat that this card suggests harmonious and happy domestic bliss. If the Cleaver family from *Leave it to Beaver* were a tarot card, they'd probably be the Ten of Cups. If you're pulling this card, things are likely going great at home, or at least you want them to be going great. We all know that even the happiest families have off days. On days when tensions are high and arguments are quick to start, working with the Ten of Cups can help bring back that loving family connection.

Ten of Cups

A Charm Spell for a Peaceful Home

Timing: Sunset

Domestic bliss can't be bottled, but you can use your magick to charm your home. In this spell, you'll work with the Ten of Cups to bring peace to your home.

What you need:

- Cleansing herb wand
- Lighter or matchbook
- Light blue tea light
- Paper and pen
- 1 tablespoon (3 g) dried lavender
- 1 tablespoon (3 g) dried olive leaves
- Ten of Cups tarot card
- Light blue envelope
- Sprinkle of vanilla extract or essential oil (diluted)

Begin by using your dried herb wand to do a thorough smoke cleanse of your home, being sure to include doorways and windows.

Light your light blue tea light and visualize a calm, happy, and peaceful home.

On the paper, draw the shape of a home. Inside the shape, write the names of all family members who live in your home, including pets if you wish, without lifting the pen (it's okay if it doesn't look perfect). Keeping the pen still on the paper, move it to the outside of the home, and write the word "peace" continually, encircling your home in peace.

Sprinkle the dried lavender, for calm, and dried olive leaves, for peace, on top of your drawing. The wax from the tea candle now should have partially melted; drip the wax over the herbs, sealing them onto your paper.

Once the wax has dried, place your spell paper, along with the Ten of Cups tarot card, inside the light blue envelope. Seal the envelope with the remaining wax from the tea candle and sprinkle a few drops of vanilla on top of the envelope, for loving and comforting energy.

Place the spell envelope under your doormat to bring peace to your home.

JOURNAL QUESTIONS:

What does a peaceful home look like? How has your family supported you? How can you better support them? What is your definition of "home"?

PAGE OF CUPS: Inspire Bright Ideas

Key words: Curiosity, possibilities, creative inspiration

Some days it just feels like the light bulb above your head is broken and no amount of flicking the light switch on and off will get it to come back on. The Page of Cups stands with a cup in hand, contemplating a fish that has appeared, and almost looks engaged in conversation with the fish. What can you take away from the Page of Cups? Stay curious to get those creative juices flowing.

Page of Cups

An Elemental Spell to Inspire That Light Bulb Moment

Timing: Sunrise, Sunday or Friday

It's vital to be open to receiving new ideas and creative inspiration. In this spell, you'll call on the elements and work with the Page of Cups to help inspire bright ideas.

What you need:

- Paper and pen
- Page of Cups tarot card
- Orange chime candle and holder
- Orange essential oil (diluted)
- Lighter or matchbook
- Light bulb (new)
- A representation of the five elements (see page 29) or crystals corresponding to each element
- Sprinkle of ground cinnamon

On your paper, draw a large pentagram; the Page of Cups card will be placed in the middle, so ensure it can fit. In the inner portion of the pentagram, write "creativity" or a word that feels aligned for you. Place the Page of Cups card on top of the word in the center of the pentagram.

Anoint your candle for inspiration by rubbing a few drops of orange essential from the wick down, to draw in bright ideas from Spirit. Place the candle on the Page of Cups card, on the lower half. Stick it to the card by lighting the bottom of the candle so the wax begins to melt and sticking it upright atop the card.

Place the light bulb, for bright ideas, on the upper half of the Page of Cups, above the candle, to draw in the energy of the candle.

Moving clockwise along the pentagram, place your Water element on the right side point and say, *I call upon the element of Water to flow ideas through me.*

Place your Fire element on the next point (bottom right) and say, *I call upon the element of Fire to kindle power and light within.*

Place your Earth representation on the next point (bottom left). Say, *I call on the element of Earth to ground me as I transmute these ideas into reality.*

Place your Air element on the next point (left) and say, *I call upon the element of Air to blow the winds of intuition to me.*

Place your Spirit representation at the top point of the pentagram. Say, *I call upon the power of Spirit to bring me spiritual connection and inspiration.*

Sprinkle cinnamon in a circle around the pentagram, surrounding it with energy and inspiration.

While the candle burns, journal, dance, listen to music, meditate–get your creative juices flowing.

After the candle has burned out, remove the spell and all idea-conjuring from your mind for the rest of the day. When you awake the next morning, bright ideas will flow. Keep the light bulb at your work space to inspire you.

JOURNAL QUESTIONS:

What inspires you? What's something you're interested in learning more about? How would your creative process change if you believed anything was possible?

KNIGHT OF CUPS: Manifest Your Dream Partner

Key words: Romance, knight in shining armor, charm

The Knight of Cups is sensitive, charming, romantic, and dreamy . . . your average knight in shining armor. It seems, though, that those partners are harder and harder to come by these days. Taking a cue from the knight's action-oriented nature, this spell aims to help the Universe speed things along if you're tired of swiping "no" on dating apps and bad first dates. Remember that when manifesting, you need to meet the Universe halfway. After you complete this spell, what actions can you take to attract your dream partner?

Knight of Cups

A Bay Leaf Poppet Spell

Timing: New moon or Friday night

In this spell, you'll work with the Knight of Cups to manifest your dream partner. Like all good things, results of this spell may take time as the Universe prepares you to meet.

What you need:

- Pink chime candle and holder
- Lighter or matchbook
- Pen
- 7 dried bay leaves
- Fresh rose with a stem
- Small cauldron or fireproof bowl
- Scissors
- Knight of Cups tarot card
- 1 tablespoon (20 g) honey

Light your pink chime candle, for love and romance, and spend two to three minutes getting clear on what your dream partner is like. What do they look like? What do they do for work? How do they treat you? What qualities that you consider important do they possess?

Pick seven of the most important things, and write each one down on a bay leaf, for manifestation and wishes. It can be just one word or an entire phrase. Remember to be specific!

Form your bay leaves into the shape of a person, with one horizontal for the head, two lengthwise for the body, and the remaining four as the arms and legs, creating a poppet.

Carefully tilt your pink candle over each leaf so the melted wax drips and binds the leaves together.

Take your rose and pick the petals off one by one and drop them into your cauldron. As you pick and drop each petal, say, *I draw my dream partner to me.*

Using the flame from the pink candle, light each bay leaf from your poppet on fire, to release your manifestation into the Universe. Hold it for as long as you're safely able, and then drop it into the cauldron to let it finish burning. If the flame goes out, simply relight it.

With scissors, cut the Knight of Cups tarot card into the shape of a heart, for romantic love, and add it to your cauldron. (If you don't want to cut your actual tarot card, you can use a photocopy or printed image of it.)

Drizzle the honey over the rose petals, Knight of Cups heart, and bay leaf ashes to add sweetness to your spell. Stir the mixture clockwise, to draw its energy to you, with the remaining stem from your rose.

Bury the cooled spell mixture near your front doorstep to attract love and manifest your dream partner.

JOURNAL QUESTIONS:

What does romance look like to you? How can you prepare yourself energetically so that you're ready to receive love when it arrives? What is your heart telling you it needs right now?

QUEEN OF CUPS: Deepen Your Self-Love

Key words: Intuition, guided by the heart, nurturing

Few figures in tarot emit that feeling of home more so than the Queen of Cups. Nurturing, kind, and intuitive, she's the one to speak to in meditation on those days you feel like you just need a hug from your mom. On tough days, the Queen of Cups will remind you of your goodness and ask you to make self-love more of a priority for your well-being. She wants to see you thriving, babe! It's time to take some of her advice and qualities to heart.

 Queen of Cups

A Cacao Elixir Spell for Self-Love

Timing: Monday or Friday

If you've been pulling this card often, think of it as your personal correspondence from the Queen of Cups. In this spell, you'll work with the Queen of Cups to deepen your self-love.

What you need:

- Milk of choice
- Cacao powder
- Honey
- Ground cinnamon
- Vanilla extract
- Mug or cup
- Dried organic rose petals
- Hand mirror
- Queen of Cups tarot card
- Journal and pen

Begin by making your self-love elixir. Heat your milk on the stovetop. While waiting for it to boil, think of a time you felt truly loved and seen.

After the milk has reached a boil, remove it from the heat. Stir in the cacao powder, for heart center activation, honey to taste for sweetness, a dash of cinnamon for warmth and passion, and a drop of vanilla for happiness and healing. There are no set ingredient amounts for this spell; use your intuition to guide you as you create it.

Stir your elixir thirteen times clockwise—the Queen of Cups is the thirteenth card in the suit of Cups—while focusing on self-love. Pour your elixir into your mug and top with a sprinkle of dried rose petals, for love.

While waiting for your self-love elixir to cool, it's time to charm your mirror. Hold the mirror in your hands with the Queen of Cups card on top of it and say,

May this mirror reflect back the beautiful witch I am within,
A new chapter in self-love shall now begin.

Close your eyes and imagine yourself as the Queen of Cups: nurturing, kind, creative, loving, and adored by others. Picture yourself on your throne by the sea. Open your eyes, remove the Queen of Cups, and look back at your reflection. What do you see? What emotions come up?

Drink your self-love elixir as you journal through your feelings. Look in the charmed mirror every day for thirteen days and say something nice about yourself out loud to complete the spell and deepen your self-love.

JOURNAL QUESTIONS:

Who can you turn to in life for support? How can you better support yourself? Would you describe yourself as a generally sensitive person? Why or why not? What is one thing you can implement this week to take better care of yourself?

KING OF CUPS: Scrub Away Stress

Key words: Balanced, wise, in control

Have you been feeling lately like you've been tossed into the ocean and are struggling to keep your head above water? Let the King of Cups throw you a life raft! The wise MacDaddy of the minor arcana, the King of Cups is the personification of calm, cool, and collected. While the sea is turbulent around him, he remains steadfast and unmoving in his calm demeanor on his solid stone throne. He's also compassionate and in touch with his emotional side; after he saves you from drowning, he'll probably make you a cup of tea, too.

King of Cups

A *Magick Salt Scrub Spell*

Timing: Waning moon

Working with the King of Cups and internalizing his energy can be helpful when you're feeling stress. In this spell, you'll work with the King of Cups to scrub away the overwhelm.

What you need:

- King of Cups tarot card
- Bowl
- Spoon
- 1 cup (224 g) Epsom salts
- ¼ cup (60 ml) jojoba oil
- 5 to 10 drops eucalyptus oil
- 1 tablespoon (3 g) dried lavender
- Airtight container

Take your spell ingredients into the bathroom. Before you create anything, stand in front of the mirror and place the King of Cups on the sink in front of you. Place your hands on the card and receive his strength and calm demeanor.

Look at yourself and, rather than seeing a person, try to see your soul reflected back. A soul who, while maybe mega stressed, is also taking time for themselves and is doing their best. Say aloud to your reflection, *I am safe. I am in control. I am okay.*

In a bowl using a spoon, mix the Epsom salts, for protection, and jojoba oil, for healing. Once those have been combined, add 5 to 10 drops of eucalyptus oil, for calm and stress release. Sprinkle in the dried lavender to help promote relaxation. Pour the magick salt scrub into an airtight container to store.

In the shower, feel the water on your skin. As the King of Cups sits steadfast on his throne while the waters swirl around him, you stand steadfast in the shower as the water moves around you.

Starting from the top of your body and working down, to dispel negative energy, gently use your magick salt scrub on your skin. Do not use salt scrub on your face.

Visualize scrubbing away your stress and overwhelm. As you hold the magick salt scrub in your hands and cleanse your body, say,

I scrub away stress, I scrub away fear,
I scrub away all unwanted energy here.
Overwhelm is washed away,
I am safe, I am in control, I am okay

Keep the magick salt scrub in your shower and use as needed to gently scrub away stress and overwhelm.

JOURNAL QUESTIONS:

What physical sensations come up in your body when you're feeling stress and overwhelm? What is one coping mechanism that's helped you work through stress in the past? Can you be more compassionate with yourself in this present moment?

ACE OF WANDS: Begin a New Project

Key words: Inspiration, new opportunities, breakthrough

Ideas can strike in the most unsuspecting places: in the shower, while you're sleeping, or when you're working out. When an idea to begin a new project strikes, think of it as a magickal tap of the wand from the Ace of Wands. A card of breakthroughs, inspiration, and opportunity, the Ace of Wands is your tarot fairy godmother, bestowing ideas upon you. And it's your job to act on them! The suit of Wands is associated with passion and action, translating the Ace of Wands to taking passionate and inspired action on your ideas.

Ace of Wands

A Seed Spell for Growth

Timing: New moon

Let's be honest, the hardest part of any new project is actually starting. In this spell, you'll work with the Ace of Wands to take the first step and begin a new project.

What you need:

- Branch or stick, about 12 inches (30 cm) long
- Gold paint
- Small piece of paper
- Seeds gathered from an apple
- Ace of Wands tarot card

Holding your branch, representative of the Ace of Wands, spend two to three minutes focusing on and visualizing the new project you're beginning. This will charge your wand with your intention.

Dip your "wand" into the gold paint, for abundance, and write down a word or phrase on your piece of paper that represents your new beginning. It can be what kind of project you're starting or a simple word such as "success."

While the paint is still wet, sprinkle your apple seeds, for growth, onto the paint. It's okay if the words become smudged or illegible. Hold both hands over your paper and say,

Today's the day I start something new,
With seeds to grow and wand for pen.
Ace of Wands, I invoke from you,
Abundance and opportunity as I begin.

Place the Ace of Wands card on top of the spell paper to charge it with Ace of Wands energy. Fold up your paper and the Ace of Wands card together, folding the edges toward yourself to draw the spell's energy to you.

Bury your spell paper and wand on the night of a new moon for prosperous and successful beginnings on your new project.

JOURNAL QUESTIONS:

What excites you about this new opportunity or project? Where do you draw inspiration from? What is one new opportunity you'll take advantage of this month?

TWO OF WANDS: Get a New Job

Key words: Expansion, future planning, discovery

The Two of Wands is that part at the beginning of a movie or book where the main character has had a revelation and is ready to change the direction of their life. Have you been through something similar recently? Perhaps you've had a personal discovery or awakening that's causing you to reevaluate everything and think, "Things need to change!" You've come so far, your priorities have shifted, and you're ready to turn dreams into actionable goals with time lines.

 Two of Wands

A Resume Spell for the Perfect Job

Timing: Waxing moon or Thursday

Oftentimes, change means finding a new career! You're ready to use your talents and creativity to serve the collective in a new and inspired way. In this spell, you'll work with the Two of Wands to channel all of that expansive progressive energy to get a new job.

What you need:

- Lighter or matchbook
- Green chime candle and holder
- Your resume or a printout of the job listing
- Green pen
- Sprinkle of dried mint
- Sprinkle of biodegradable gold glitter
- 4 dried bay leaves
- Two of Wands tarot card

Light your green chime candle, for abundance, and set it in the candle holder. The flame represents the guiding light of your self-discovery, lighting new pathways and opportunities for you.

Place your resume or job listing on your work space. Using your green pen, for prosperity, continuously write the phrase "I have the perfect new job" without lifting your pen. Start at the top of your paper and write along every side, creating a border until you get back to the beginning. Still without lifting your pen, move to the center of the paper and sign your name.

The candle should now have a bit of melted wax at the top. Carefully drip some wax in a circle with about a 6-inch (15-cm) radius onto the center of your paper. Sprinkle the mint, associated with luck and money, on top of the wax before it cools.

Next, sprinkle on gold glitter, representing your best self shining through for potential interviews and clients. Place one bay leaf pointing toward each direction along the mint and gold circle, for manifestation from every direction.

Drip some wax into the center of the circle and use it to secure your green chime candle onto the spell. As the candle burns, visualize yourself in your new job. What is your salary? What do you wear to work? What does your commute look like? Get specific!

Let the candle burn out and keep the spell at your altar next to the Two of Wands card. Revisit your spell and do the visualization exercise daily until you get your new job.

JOURNAL QUESTIONS:

What have you learned about yourself recently that has made you realize you've outgrown where you are? What are your long-term goals? How will this new expansive version of you change the world?

THREE OF WANDS: Clear the Road Ahead

Key words: Exploration, progress, looking ahead

You've got your plans to take over the world all set, and you're standing at the front steps of your house, backpack and walking shoes on, looking out at the long road ahead. Oh wait . . . you're sitting in a comfy chair, reading this (amazing) book? Well, if your life was a movie based on your tarot deck, that first part of the paragraph–that's where you'd be according to the Three of Wands. You've got big plans in the mix and are about to embark on something new. A new job, relationship, move, chapter of your life–whatever it is for you, you're ready to begin!

Three of Wands

A Road-Clearing Spell for New Beginnings

Timing: Full moon or sunrise

It can't hurt to have some extra magick on your side as you embark on this new journey. In this spell, you'll work with the Three of Wands to clear the road ahead.

What you need:

- Lighter or matchbook
- Raspberry incense and holder
- Orange peel
- Black marker
- Small obsidian crystal
- Yellow ribbon, 12 inches (30 cm) long
- Three of Wands tarot card

Light your raspberry incense, for removing obstacles, and visualize the smoke clearing the path ahead for you.

Using a sweeping motion with your dominant hand, clear the smoke from in front of you three times, and say, *I clear the road ahead.*

On an orange peel, associated with opening opportunities, use a black marker to sign your name and the day's date. Place an obsidian crystal, for removing obstacles, inside the orange peel, and tie it closed using your yellow ribbon, a main color in the Three of Wands card.

Take your orange peel spell and the Three of Wands card to a crossroads (a place where two or more roads meet). Bury your spell at the crossroads to clear the road ahead.

Pick up a handful of crossroads dirt and sprinkle it over the Three of Wands to charm your card. As you sprinkle the dirt, say,

The road ahead is clear for me,
I charm you now, my Wands of Three.
Keep my path open wide,
Whichever direction I choose, the road abides.

Blow the dirt off toward the South. The South is associated with the element of Fire, which corresponds to the suit of Wands.

Keep your charmed Three of Wands card with you as you continue on your journey and the road ahead.

JOURNAL QUESTIONS:

Where will you be in six months? In one year? What systems do you have in place to draw support from when things get difficult? Are you ready to move past your comfort zone?

FOUR OF WANDS: Bring Happiness to Your Home

Key words: Happy home, celebration, family

While you can't live *every* day like you're throwing a party, with the Four of Wands, you can at least work with that happy energy! A card of joy, homecoming, and family, the Four of Wands encourages you to "forget your troubles, come on, get happy," like Judy Garland says, and celebrate yourself where you're at. It's difficult to cultivate that energy in a home with a less-than-cheery atmosphere, though. When was the last time you worked your magick to bring happiness to your home?

Four of Wands

A Rose Quartz Spell for a Happy Home

Timing: Sunday or sunrise

It's easier to celebrate and feel truly at home in a space with good energy. In this spell, you'll work with the Four of Wands to bring happiness to your home. This spell is best done when you're home alone.

What you need:

- Music that evokes happiness
- Bowl of water
- Four of Wands tarot card
- Number of small rose quartz pieces to correspond with number of rooms in your home (e.g., 4 rooms, 4 pieces)
- Pen
- 1 dried bay leaf
- 1 tablespoon (5 g) dried basil
- Petals from 1 sunflower
- A few drops of vanilla extract or essential oil (diluted)
- 1 tablespoon (3 g) dried rose petals (a few drops of rose essential oil or rosewater can also be used)

Set the mood by playing music that makes you happy! Put it on loud to get into it, and so you can hear it throughout the house. Go through your home and open all the windows and doors to let the stale energy exit–make sure pets cannot get out! You can do a room-by-room smoke cleanse of your house at this point in the spell.

Return to your work space and set the bowl of water in front of you, on top of the Four of Wands tarot card to charge the water. Drop in one rose quartz piece at a time. As you place it in the bowl, say aloud the corresponding room in your home.

Once all of the rose quartz pieces have been placed in the bowl, write "happy home" on your bay leaf and add it to the bowl. Add the dried basil and the petals of one sunflower for happiness, and vanilla for peace.

Sprinkle in the rose petals for loving energy. Stir the happy home potion clockwise with your fingers to draw happy energy to your home.

Go room to room in your home, and using your fingers, sprinkle the happy home potion in the corners, doorways, and windows of each room. As you do so, say,

My home is blessed and filled with happiness.

Leave one rose quartz piece somewhere in each room (out of reach of any small children or pets) before you exit it, as a talisman of happiness.

Use any remaining happy home potion to water flowers or pour it outside your front door to complete the spell and bring happiness to your home.

JOURNAL QUESTIONS:

What does "home" feel like to you? Is it a physical place? A person? A feeling? What do you have to celebrate and be happy about in this very moment? Write a thank-you letter to your house.

FIVE OF WANDS: Repair a Friendship

Key words: Quarrel, conflict, tension

Having disagreements and getting into fights are some of the less fun parts of friendship. The Five of Wands reflects a time of disagreement or competition, and the tension in the room is so thick it could be sliced with your athame. Now isn't the time to let your ego call the shots. Instead, step back, take a deep breath, and try to see things from the other person's viewpoint. Is there a way you can get back on the same page? Or better understand the page they're on? In Five of Wands situations, the best way to end the conflict is to put down your wand and pick up an olive branch.

Five of Wands

A *Friendship Bracelet Spell*

Timing: Full moon, new moon, or noon

Are you asking yourself what you can do to repair the damage that's been done to a relationship? In this spell, you'll work with the Five of Wands to repair a friendship.

What you need:

- Five of Wands tarot card
- Light blue chime candle and holder
- Toothpick or safety pin to carve candle
- A few drops of olive oil
- Lighter or matchbook
- 3 pieces of string or ribbon, 12 to 16 inches (30 to 41 cm) long, in your friend's favorite colors
- Scissors
- Light purple sachet
- Moonstone crystal

•••••••••••••••••••••••••••••••••••••

Because you're casting this spell with a friend in mind, begin by declaring out loud,

I cast this spell to repair my friendship with (friend's name). I ask this energy be delivered to them only if they are open and willing to receive it. When working with the energy of others, it's important to state that you only want your spell to be delivered if the other party is open and receptive to it. You always want to respect the free will of others.

•••••••••••••••••••••••••••••••••••••

Set the Five of Wands card in the reversed position, indicating ending conflict, on your work space.

Take your blue candle, associated with peace, and use a toothpick to carve the names of both you and the friend you're aiming to repair the friendship with. Initials will work, too.

Anoint your candle with olive oil, for peace, by rubbing a few drops of olive oil on your fingers and rubbing it onto the candle from the bottom to the top, sending the peaceful energy out into the Universe to your friend. Light the candle.

As the candle burns, take your three cords and tie them together in a knot at one end. Braid the cords together until they are the length of a bracelet. As you braid, think of your friend and how much you care for them. Visualize a warm white light surrounding the cord as you braid and charge it with your loving intentions. Once you've reached the desired length, tie another knot and cut off the excess cord.

Place the bracelet in the light purple sachet, a color associated with harmony, along with the moonstone crystal, for reconciliation. Hold your spell sachet to your heart and say,

Our broken friendship, I ask to repair,
May this peace offering clear the air.
If it's meant to be,
We'll live once again in harmony.

Let the candle burn down and set the melted wax on top of the reversed Five of Wands card on your altar. Give the spell sachet to your friend as a peace offering to repair your friendship.

JOURNAL QUESTIONS:

How can you work or interact more harmoniously with others? Is it worth it to "win" in this situation? Or, are you putting your ego ahead of relationships? How does your competitive nature play into disagreements?

SIX OF WANDS: Get Noticed at Work

Key words: Recognition, leadership, success

Passed over for that promotion *again*? Maybe you put in extra hours but your boss didn't seem to notice. Or you took the lead on a project and didn't receive acknowledgment. It's never a fun place to be when others don't seem to notice your accomplishments. The Six of Wands is a card of that magick formula that makes you feel on top of the world: achievement plus acknowledgment. It's your personal "Yay for me!" parade, celebrating your accomplishments and growth.

Six of Wands

A Sun Water Spray to Get You Noticed

Timing: Waxing moon

If you've been putting in the effort but haven't been getting noticed by others, the Six of Wands is a great card to work with. In this spell, you'll work with the Six of Wands to get noticed at work.

What you need:

- Small glass spray bottle
- Six of Wands tarot card
- Lighter or matchbook
- Red chime candle and holder
- 6 small pieces of paper
- Red pen
- Small cauldron or fireproof bowl
- Tiger's eye crystal

Fill the spray bottle with water and leave it outside or on a windowsill that gets sunlight for six hours, with the Six of Wands card underneath to charge it with leadership and victory. Sun water carries properties of illumination, strength, and healing.

Once your sun water has been made, bring it, along with the Six of Wands card, to your work space. Light a red chime candle, for power and attention. Spend two to three minutes focusing on the flame. Visualize its brightness illuminating you and your hard work in the eyes of others.

On one piece of paper, with red pen, write, "I am noticed. My work is appreciated." Spray the paper with a quick spritz of sun water, and light it on fire with the flame of the candle. Drop it into the cauldron to burn safely and hold the tiger's eye in an open hand above it as it burns to charge it with your spell's intentions. Tiger's eye is a flashy stone with properties that help you get noticed, draw the spotlight to you, and strengthen your confidence in your personal power.

Extinguish the candle. Add a spritz of sun water to a drink every day to further embody the sun's properties.

Repeat the spell every day for a total of six days, and on the sixth day scatter the combined ashes into the South, the direction of Fire, the element associated with the suit of Wands. Carry the tiger's eye with you while at work to get noticed.

JOURNAL QUESTIONS:

What does success look like or mean to you? How do the attention and admiration of others play into your self-confidence? What is your personal power? Which of your abilities are you confident about?

SEVEN OF WANDS: Knock
Out the Competition

Key words: Challenges, competition, opposition

Put on the gloves, Rocky, because it's about to go down! The Seven of Wands suggests you're either in a position envied by others or are competing for something. This card reminds you to draw upon your inner strength and self-belief, and not let anything get in the way of your goals, ambitions, and dreams. One aspect of this card suggests being caught off guard by the opposition of others, so it's vital that you take time to prepare and arm yourself before walking into the ring–good thing you've got this book!

Seven of Wands

A Wand Spell to Defeat Competitors

Timing: Waning moon

Battling it out to stand your ground or beat out the rest can be tough. In this spell, you'll work with the Seven of Wands to knock out the competition.

What you need:

- Seven of Wands tarot card
- Bowl of water
- 7 small sticks, 2 to 3 inches (5 to 7.5 cm) long
- 1 tablespoon (15 ml) lemon juice

Set the Seven of Wands tarot card in front of the bowl of water. Separate one small stick from the rest and place the other six on top of the Seven of Wands card.

Add the lemon juice to the water, to sour the efforts of your competitors.

Hold one stick in the palm of your dominant hand and close your first around it. This represents your wand, what you use to knock out the competition.

In the hand holding the stick, knock on the table while using the other hand to toss a stick in the water, knocking and tossing six total times as you chant,

One to sour,
Two to rise above,
Three to overpower,
Four to dispose of,
Five to never doubt,
Six to knock my competition out.

Feel the seventh and last remaining wand in your hand and visualize yourself knocking out your competition.

Remove the sticks from the water and pour it down the sink, then throw the sticks in a compostable trash bin.

Carry your wand with you during the competition or competitive time period to knock out your competition.

JOURNAL QUESTIONS:

What is your relationship to self-confidence? How do you react when challenged? Are you ready and willing to fight for yourself? How can you be a better teammate to yourself?

EIGHT OF WANDS:
Speed Things Up

Key words: Movement, rapid change, speed

Prepare for liftoff, babe, because you're ready to become airborne! Every cell in your body is screaming, "GO!" and your feet are anxiously tapping while you wait for things to finally get set into motion. The Eight of Wands is a card of movement and motion. If you're ready and raring to go but are feeling frustrated with the lack of speed with which things are moving, this is the card to work with.

 Eight of Wands

A Cinnamon Spell for Speed

Timing: Tuesday

In this spell, you'll work with the Eight of Cups to speed things up. One thing to remember as you work with the Eight of Wands: With swift movement comes swift change. Be aware of potential effects and consequences that hastening things up may have.

What you need:

- Cup of coffee or other caffeinated drink
- Cinnamon stick
- Pen
- Representation of what you are trying to speed up (e.g., a coin for money, a rose for love, resume for a job, etc.)
- Lighter or matchbook
- Small cauldron or fireproof bowl
- Sprinkle of cayenne pepper
- Eight of Wands tarot card

As you prepare your coffee, focus on your intentions for the spell. Stir the coffee clockwise three times to stir your intention into the drink. Take the first sip and feel the coffee in your body, invigorating every cell.

On the cinnamon stick, write down a word or phrase that represents what you want to speed up. Light one end of the cinnamon, associated with speed, on fire. When you see a flame, blow it out so the stick begins to smoke. You may need to do this a few times before achieving a good amount of smoke.

Hold your representation in one hand and move the cinnamon stick around it, fully engulfing the representation in smoke. As you do so, say,

Haste is made, things move with speed,
Ready, set, go, now quickly proceed.

Place the cinnamon stick and representation in your cauldron. Sprinkle cayenne on top for further acceleration. Set the Eight of Wands card under the cauldron to charge the spell with movement.

Finish drinking your coffee and spend this time visualizing the results you want from the spell.

Bury the cooled ingredients near a weed (for quick growth) and keep the Eight of Wands with you as you work to speed things up.

JOURNAL QUESTIONS:

How can you direct your energy in a more focused manner? What is the current path you're headed down? Are there potential consequences for moving things along too quickly?

NINE OF WANDS: Protect Yourself from Bad Vibes

Key words: Challenges, battle, resilience

Like a crowded karaoke bar on Saturday night, the hits just keep on coming. Unlike a karaoke bar, though, the hits you're being dealt aren't pop songs; they're obstacles, delays, and challenges. Way less fun. The Nine of Wands has you feeling battered and bruised and on the brink of giving up. Here's the thing about this card, though: Although you're exhausted, the Nine of Wands reminds you that you're a resilient, badass babe! Drawing the Nine of Wands means you're *so close* to relief. You've got this!

Nine of Wands

A Spell to Create a Circle of Protection

Timing: Waning moon

You may be tired, but you're not ready to give up. You just need a little extra magick protection to keep going. Dust yourself off, do a spell to protect yourself from the bad vibes, and keep pushing.

What you need:

- Black pen
- Paper
- 9 iron nails
- 1 tablespoon (15 g) salt
- Nine of Wands tarot card

Begin by taking three deep breaths and envisioning a protective light surrounding you and your magick tools, growing bigger and stronger with each breath.

With your black pen, draw a large pentacle in the center of your paper. The pentacle can be a protective sigil, and the five points of the star represent the five elements: Earth, Air, Fire, Water, and Spirit.

In the middle of the pentacle, write your name. As you write your name, visualize being supported and protected by universal energy. Picture the wands of the Nine of Wands not as weapons that will further knock you down, but rather as beams creating a protective barrier between you and any bad vibes coming your way.

Place an iron nail, a protective talisman, at the top of each star point, encircling the pentacle. Place the remaining four nails surrounding your name.

Encompass the pentacle and nails with a circle of salt, as one last protective layer. Set the Nine of Wands card above your spell paper, symbolizing rising above any negative energy thrown your way.

Place both of your hands over your spell and say aloud,

Pentacle of nails, and circle of salt,
protect me now, and bad vibes halt.

Keep your spell on your altar and refresh it with more salt when you need extra protection.

JOURNAL QUESTIONS:

What boundaries do you need to uphold more strongly in your life? What waits for you at the finish line? What is a source of inner strength you can draw from in times of defeat?

TEN OF WANDS: Call on Strength from the Universe

Key words: Pushing your limits, uphill battle, overloaded

Yikes, babe. Could the load you're carrying on your shoulders be any heavier? You're facing a tough battle right now, and things feel more difficult with each step. The Ten of Wands is a card of hard work and pushing yourself to the limit. Did your grandpa ever tell you the story of how he had to walk barefoot uphill both ways in the snow to get to school? Grandpa was giving off some serious Ten of Wands energy. Whether you're taking on extra shifts at work, courses in school, or the emotional responsibility of others, the Ten of Wands suggests feeling close to being burnt out. The positive about this card, though, is that it suggests an end is in sight!

Ten of Wands

An Offering Spell to Ask for Strength

Timing: Full moon or Saturday

You're so close to the end, you just need to keep going. And that's when your magick comes in. In this spell, you'll work with the Ten of Wands to call on strength from the Universe.

What you need:

- Pen
- Ten of Wands tarot card
- 1 scoop protein powder
- Small cauldron or fireproof bowl
- Lighter or matchbook
- Fresh flowers or fruit as an offering to the Universe

Begin by practicing deep breathing for one minute to slow down your central nervous system and sink into a more relaxed state.

With a pen on the Ten of Wands tarot card, write down what you need assistance with or strength for from the Universe. If you don't want to use the card from your deck, a photocopy of the card will work.

Take your scoop of protein powder, for strength, and sprinkle it into the shape of the Gebo rune (looks like an X), symbolizing generosity and giving, on your work space. The shape of the Gebo rune also closely resembles the shape the wands form in the Ten of Wands card in the Rider-Waite-Smith illustration.

Place the cauldron inside the top opening of the Gebo. Light the Ten of Wands card on fire and place it into the cauldron to burn, releasing your request to the Universe. As it burns, say,

Universe, I call on your aid,
Lend me strength in the coming days.

As the smoke rises, visualize your request being sent to the Universe and received as it disappears.

Set fresh flowers or fruit in the bottom opening of the Gebo as an offering of thanks to the Universe for aiding in your request for strength.

Replace the offering every few days for as long as you want to keep the spell active to call on aid from the Universe.

JOURNAL QUESTIONS:

Is there a way for you to lighten the load you're carrying? Do your current responsibilities feel like a burden? What can you do to relieve stress at this time?

PAGE OF WANDS: Communicate Clearly

Key words: Spreading news and messages, energetic, enthusiastic

Like an easily excitable town crier, the Page of Wands brings passionate and energetic communication to the mix. The Page of Wands manifests new beginnings and brings plans and ideas to fruition. When this energy isn't flowing in your life, things can get mega frustrating. Being unable to get your truth across can cause tension, conflict, stalled ideas, and exasperation. Working with the Page of Wands can be effective for improving communication at work or with a partner, public speaking, or just overall learning how to express yourself.

Page of Wands

A Magick Snack Mix for Clear Communication

Timing: Wednesday

In this spell, you'll work with the Page of Wands to communicate clearly in any situation.

What you need:

- Lighter or matchbook
- Yellow chime candle and holder
- Sodalite crystal
- Airtight container
- ½ cup (60 g) dried cranberries
- ½ cup (73 g) sunflower seeds
- ½ cup (60 g) chopped walnuts
- ¼ cup (44 g) dark chocolate chips
- Page of Wands tarot card

Light a yellow chime candle and place it in a candle holder. Yellow is a color associated with clear communication. Hold a sodalite crystal over the candle as you picture yourself communicating with grace, clarity, and ease to charge the crystal with your intention. Sodalite aids in opening the energy of the throat, helping you clearly speak your truth and communicate. Set the sodalite next to the candle.

In an airtight container, combine the dried cranberries for communication, sunflower seeds for confidence, walnuts to improve intelligence and connection to your brain, and dark chocolate chips for relaxation. Close the lid, gently shake the mix, and say,

Communication comes easy and clear,
I speak my truth and others hear.

Drip some yellow wax onto the outside of the lid to seal the container. Extinguish the candle. Place the Page of Wands card and the crystal on the lid to charge.

When you want to ensure you communicate clearly, place the sodalite in your pocket and have a few bites of the clear communication snack mix to improve your communication.

••

A Magick Snack Mix to Improve Communication Between You and Another Person

If you want to improve the communication between you and someone else specifically, add these steps and items to the spell.

- Pen
- 2 small pieces of paper
- Needle
- White thread
- Small zip-top bag

Write down your name on one piece of paper and the person you wish to improve communication with on the other.

Thread a needle with white thread, then pierce it through both papers and tie together. The circle of thread represents clear and open communication between the two of you and an equal exchange of energy.

Place the names and thread in a zip-top bag and put the bag in the container of clear communication snack mix. Take a few bites of the mix before having a conversation with the other person to improve communication between the two of you.

••

JOURNAL QUESTIONS:

Do you have trouble expressing yourself? Has there ever been a time when someone else heard something other than what you were trying to get across? What likely caused the mix-up in communication? What opportunities are available to you if you can express yourself truthfully and fully?

KNIGHT OF WANDS: Be Bold and Courageous

Key words: Confidence, power, fearlessness

Look at you, babe! Feeling bold, inspired, and ready to take on whatever life throws at you in pursuit of your dream! The Knight of Wands calls on you to act with boldness and courage–no cowardly lion energy here! Only lion-after-he's-been-gifted-courage-by-the-great-and-powerful-Oz energy welcome around these parts. Unfortunately, most of us don't have a wizard behind a curtain to remind us of our boldness and courage when needed. But what if you could create liquid courage? No, not that kind. The magick spell kind.

Knight of Wands

A Sun-Charged Spell Oil for Courage

Timing: Tuesday or full moon

See if you can bottle up some of that post-Oz visit cowardly lion courage and keep it in your back pocket. In this spell, you'll work with the Knight of Wands to be bold and courageous.

What you need:

- Black permanent marker
- Small glass jar
- Carnelian crystal
- ¼ cup (60 ml) sunflower oil
- Sprinkle of black pepper
- 3 whole cloves
- 1 teaspoon dried thyme
- Pine essential oil
- Optional: biodegradable glitter in gold, orange, or red
- Knight of Wands tarot card

Begin by creating a sigil for boldness and courage (see page 18). Using a black permanent marker for strength, draw your sigil on the outside of the glass jar.

Place a piece of carnelian in the jar. Carnelian aids in helping you embody your courage, stimulate your power, and generate fearlessness.

Next, add the sunflower oil. Sunflower oil is the chosen carrier for this spell blend because it contains properties of self-confidence and positivity. Sprinkle in black pepper and add the three cloves for protection, dried thyme for courage, and a few drops of pine essential oil for grounding and resilience.

If you like working with glitter, sprinkle in gold, orange, or red biodegradable glitter. These colors correspond with the suit of Wands.

Place the lid on the jar and gently turn it upside down and right-side up a few times to mix the ingredients.

Set your spell oil in the sun for a few hours to charge with the sun's properties of courage and strength.

Once you've brought your spell oil inside, anoint the Knight of Wands tarot card with your spell oil and keep it in your back pocket on days you need to summon your inner boldness and courageousness. When you're walking into a situation in which you feel uneasy or intimidated, be comforted by the fact that you've got courage in your back pocket.

Additionally, use the spell oil to anoint your heart space, hands, and feet to further absorb the properties of the spell oil.

JOURNAL QUESTIONS:

What are you excited about pursuing or working toward? How can you be bolder in your approach? What fears do you need to overcome or work through to pursue your dream or passion?

QUEEN OF WANDS: Relieve Social Anxiety

Key words: Friend, leadership, sociability

Be honest, are you the person at the party who's hanging out in the corner petting the dog and avoiding making eye contact with everyone else there? Social anxiety can be difficult! As adults, and as witches, we tend to get lost in our own worlds, and when we finally come up for air, socializing again can be intimidating. The creative, social butterfly of the tarot deck, the Queen of Wands is passionate, outgoing, and confident. She asks you to fully believe in your amazing, wonderful, kind, and creative self, and put yourself out there! We're talking main character energy here.

Queen of Wands

A Sachet Spell for Anxiety

Timing: Afternoon or Sunday

Not that it's a bad thing to be in your own world, but sometimes it's important to be social, too! In this spell, you'll work with the Queen of Wands to relieve social anxiety.

What you need:

- Lighter or matchbook
- Orange tea light
- Ice cube
- Queen of Wands tarot card
- 2 small bowls
- Dry rice (to fill your small orange sachet two-thirds full)
- Lemon essential oil (diluted)
- Spoon
- Small orange sachet
- Howlite crystal
- Lepidolite crystal
- Amethyst crystal
- Skillet

Light an orange tea light, for confidence, courage, strength, and relationships. Hold an ice cube in one hand and the Queen of Wands card in the other.

Close your eyes and concentrate on the social anxiety you're feeling. Visualize the social anxiety leaving your body and transferring into the ice cube.

Set the ice cube in a small bowl near the orange tea light and place the Queen of Wands card next to it. As the ice cube melts while you complete the rest of your spell, it symbolically melts away your anxiety.

Next, add your dry rice to the second bowl. Add a few drops of diluted lemon essential oil to the rice and stir with a spoon. Lemon oil is energizing and uplifting and promotes friendship.

Pour the rice into the orange sachet. Add the howlite, lepidolite, and amethyst crystals; all are ideal crystals to work with when relieving anxiety. Extinguish the candle.

Your orange sachet should now feel like a small weight. Weights help provide comfort during anxiety-inducing situations. Keep the sachet with you in your pocket or purse and hold or fidget with it when you're in social situations.

For the last step of the spell, pour the melted ice, symbolizing your anxiety, into a skillet and place it over the heat on the stovetop so the water evaporates, completely eliminating your social anxiety

JOURNAL QUESTIONS:

When was the last time you felt extremely confident and in your element? In what ways do you express yourself creatively? How comfortable are you sharing that side of yourself with others? What are you feeling passionate about right now?

KING OF WANDS: Gain Control of a Situation

Key words: Power, mastery, leadership

The King of Wands walks into a room with swagger and commands everyone's attention. His confidence and mastery over situations make him a natural-born leader. In the land of real life, things don't always work out in the bold, powerful way of the King of Wands. Bills pile up, a blowup happens with a friend, you get behind at work . . . things just snowball. When that happens, it's time to put your crown on and call on the King of Wands to assist you.

King of Wands

A Poppet Spell for Control

Timing: Tuesday or Saturday

Sometimes a situation spirals out of control and you feel you have no way to get hold of it again. In this spell, you'll work with the King of Wands to gain control of a situation.

What you need:

- Lighter or matchbook
- Red chime candle and holder
- King chess piece (black or white, whichever you prefer)
- 1 teaspoon red paint
- Paper and pen
- Scissors
- Red string, about 24 inches (61 cm) long
- King of Wands tarot card

Light a red chime candle for power, action, boldness, and control.

In this spell, the king chess piece represents you embodying the King of Wands. Dip your thumb in red paint and roll it across the center of the king chess piece, putting a personal touch on the chess piece that's unique to you and combining your energies.

On a small square of paper, write the situation that you want to gain control over. Poke a small hole on each of the four sides of the paper. Cut a piece of red string into four equal pieces; red is a color associated with power. Tie one piece of string to each corner. You've now made a marionette puppet from the situation: You hold the strings and can control it.

Gather the four ends of the strings and place them over your thumbprint on the king chess piece. Carefully drip wax from the red chime candle over the strings, sealing them to the chess piece. Extinguish the candle.

Now the situation is attached to you and can be controlled by you. Hold the spell in one hand and the King of Wands card in the other and say,

The situation is mine to control:
I decide that the outcome matches my goal.
It's mine to move and pull the string,
Spell in hand, I am the king.

It's up to you to decide how to use the spell from here. Place your spell in the situation you want to control. For example, to control spending, set the spell on top of a dollar bill or on your wallet. To control the outcome of a test, set the spell on top of your textbook. To gain control of a family situation, set the spell on a picture of your family. Get creative with the placement of your spell poppet and how you use it.

JOURNAL QUESTIONS:

How do you feel when you're in control of a situation? How do you feel when you're not? What kind of leadership qualities do you have? Do your actions match your words, or do you tend to be big talk and no action?

ACE OF SWORDS: Have Your Breakthrough Moment

Key words: Breakthrough, mental clarity, focus

In cartoons, you see it as the light bulb that appears over a character's head as they shout, "Eureka!" Have you ever had one of those moments where suddenly the pieces fall into place, and things just *make sense*? That's your Ace of Swords moment! You can imagine a little Ace of Swords tarot card hovering over your head when the flash of mental clarity strikes. The Ace of Swords brings focus and success; whatever your breakthrough moment is, it'll be one that ends in achievement and victory. Not too shabby, Ace!

Ace of Swords

A Smoke-Scrying Spell for Clarity

Timing: Noon or full moon

When things feel like you're driving through the fog and you can't quite see clearly, that's when you work with this card. In this spell, you'll work with the Ace of Swords to have your breakthrough moment.

••

Scrying is a form of divination in which you look into a medium (in our case, smoke) for messages or visions. To practice smoke scrying, make sure you're seated in a comfortable position. Let your eyes follow the smoke, and notice pictures or visions that appear.

••

What you need:

- Binaural beats music
- Lighter or matchbook
- Sandalwood incense and holder
- Paper and pen
- Full tarot deck, including Ace of Swords

Put on binaural beats music for focus and concentration. Working with binaural beats can be helpful In spellwork because they can help your mind tap into a more meditative and creative state.

Light sandalwood incense, for clarity. Close your eyes and focus on the situation or circumstance in which you're seeking a breakthrough. Say,

Through smoke the air is clear,
What I need for my breakthrough, I see here.

Open your eyes and use the incense smoke for smoke scrying. Write down each form as you see it. Because smoke is continuously moving, you don't need to fixate on one spot, let your eyes shift with the smoke. Some people even relax their vision a bit so that it's less focused. Do whatever feels right for you in the moment.

When you feel that the scrying is complete after a few minutes, shuffle your tarot deck, focusing on your intention and breakthrough as you hold the cards.

Find the Ace of Swords. The card behind it is what you're not seeing about the situation, and the card in front is what the Universe is illuminating to you. Write these cards down with your scrying notes.

What needs to be revealed to you for your breakthrough is within your findings during this spell. Put together any patterns, repeating messages, or aha instances to find your breakthrough moment.

JOURNAL QUESTIONS:

Why do you feel your breakthrough moment has been evading you? What action can you take to start moving forward from here? What is your intuition telling you about this new beginning?

TWO OF SWORDS: Make the Right Choice

Feeling like you're caught between two options and unsure of the path to take? The Two of Swords illustrates this dilemma perfectly. A card of choices, the Two of Swords is a card of weighing what appear to be two equal paths. This card asks you to pause and check in with your intuition before continuing. Is there anything about the situation that you may not be seeing?

Two of Swords

A Coin Spell for Decision-Making

Timing: Noon

Feeling stuck in the middle? Turning to your craft can be helpful in making an empowered decision. In this spell, you'll work with the Two of Swords to make the right choice.

What you need:

- A few drops of almond oil
- Black chime candle and holder
- White chime candle and holder
- Lighter or matchbook
- Piece of paper
- 2 silver coins
- Toothpick or safety pin
- Small drawstring bag
- Two of Swords tarot card
- Optional: wax paper

Use the almond oil to anoint the black and white chime candles, rubbing the oil from top to bottom three times on each candle, to draw the wisdom of the Universe down to you. Almond oil is associated with the element of Air, which corresponds with the suit of Swords, and it also aids in providing wisdom.

Light the candles and set them in their holders. In your mind, ascribe each option you're weighing to the candles. One choice is the white candle, and one choice is the black candle.

Lay a piece of paper on your work space to protect it from hot wax. Place your silver coins on the paper. Silver is associated with the element of Air and aids in clarity of thought to help you make the right choice.

Pick up the white candle, and drip wax so that it's completely covering the side of one silver coin. Do the same with the black candle and the second coin. Once the wax has dried, flip the coins over and repeat the process, so one coin is completely covered in white wax, and the other completely covered in black wax. Recycle the paper.

Using a toothpick or safety pin, write a word or symbol in the wax that connects each coin to the option you ascribed to it earlier in the spell. For example, if you are choosing whether to leave your job, and you ascribed the black candle as staying and white as leaving, write "stay" on the black coin and "leave" on the white coin.

Drop the coins into the drawstring bag. Shake the bag three times and say,

Once for clarity,
Twice magick applied,
Three for good luck, help me decide.

Focus on your intention and look at the Two of Swords card. Ask your guides to be with you as you reach your hand in and draw out a coin.

What is your immediate reaction when you see which coin you've drawn? If you're glad, you know that's the right choice. If you're disappointed, you know you should go with the other choice.

Optional: Wrap your chosen coin in wax paper and keep it with you as a good luck charm.

JOURNAL QUESTIONS:

Why do you feel torn about this decision? What's the worst-case outcome with each option? How does each option feel in your body? Do you get nervous butterflies, tight shoulders, short of breath? What might these physical sensations mean?

THREE OF SWORDS: Mend Your Broken Heart

Key words: Pain, heartbreak, grief

Has the Heartbreak Hotel got you on its list of long-term guests lately? The Three of Swords is a card of pain, sadness, and heartbreak . . . all the makings of a good country breakup song. While it's likely difficult to be knee-deep in these emotions, the Three of Swords teaches that it's important to allow yourself to feel whatever sadness is washing over you to avoid being overwhelmed and drowned by it.

 Three of Swords

A Sewing Spell to Heal Heartbreak

Timing: Waxing moon or Friday

The Three of Swords is a great card to work with as you acknowledge, navigate, and move through heartbreak. In this spell, you'll work with the Three of Swords to mend your broken heart. Note: This spell is best performed when you're feeling ready to move through the eye of the heartbreak storm and come out the other side.

What you need:

- Scissors
- Square of red cloth, 6 × 6 inches (15 × 15 cm)
- White thread
- Needle
- ½ teaspoon salt
- ½ teaspoon dried chamomile
- 3 nails
- Bandage
- Black permanent marker
- Three of Swords tarot card

With scissors, cut out a heart from the red cloth to represent your heart. Hold the scissors in both hands and allow yourself to think back on the heartbreak you have been through. Cut the heart down the middle, to symbolize your heartbreak.

Hold the white thread in both hands. White is a color of purity and new beginnings. Using the thread and needle, sew the heart back together. As you're sewing, shift your thoughts to the future: What amazing things are you manifesting? What new adventures are in store for you in this next chapter of your life? With each stitch, sew these positive intentions and healing thoughts into the heart.

Once the heart has been sewn back together, sprinkle salt on it to protect yourself from future heartbreak, then sprinkle it with the chamomile, an herb that aids in healing. Place the nails in the center of the heart, signifying the Three of Swords, and the resilience newly found as you navigate this heartbreak.

On the bandage, write the word "healed" with black marker. Roll up the heart with the ingredients inside, being sure to roll toward yourself as you draw healing inward, and wrap the bandage around it to keep it sealed into a roll. As you wrap the bandage around it, say,

A heart once broken now is healed,
Mended with a brand-new shield.
Three of Swords, my sadness moves away,
Whole again in the new day.

Place the heart on top of the Three of Swords card in its reversed position, signifying healing, next to your bed (being careful that the ingredients don't slip out the top or bottom) for one night.

The next day, bury the heart near running water, to signify cleansing, to mend your broken heart.

JOURNAL QUESTIONS:

What has this heartbreak taught you? Have you caused any hurt in this situation? What has this experience forever changed about you?

FOUR OF SWORDS: Slow Things Down

Key words: Rest, recharging, contemplation

If your guides were watching your life with a remote control in hand, about now is when they'd be frantically hitting the "pause" button, hoping you receive the message. The Four of Swords is a card of rest, taking a moment to sit in stillness before moving forward again. You know those times when you're feeling distressed in the evening, and you wake up and things suddenly feel a bit better in the morning? That's some Four of Swords action right there!

 Four of Swords

A Freezer Spell to Slow Things Down

Timing: Midnight

Sometimes it can feel as if things are moving too quickly, and you're unable to jump off the speeding train that is your life. During those times, use the Four of Swords to pump the brakes so you can rest and gain a clearer perspective. In this spell, you'll work with the Four of Swords to slow things down.

What you need:

- Paper and pen
- Small glass jar with lid
- Rubber band
- Snail shell (collected ethically) or representation of a snail
- Four of Swords tarot card
- 1 to 2 tablespoons (20 to 40 g) molasses
- Lighter or matchbook
- Yellow chime candle and holder

Begin by focusing on what you want to slow down. Write it down on a piece of paper and drop it in the jar.

Add a rubber band, to symbolize the elasticity of time, and stretching it out when you need to. Add the snail shell, or picture of a snail, to represent a slow-moving pace.

Drop in the Four of Swords tarot card, representing rest and taking a break (fold the card, if necessary). Last, drizzle the molasses, sticky and slow moving, over everything inside the jar.

Put on the lid and light a yellow chime candle. Yellow is the color that means to "slow down" at stop lights, so we're adding it to the jar as a further slowing down element.

Seal the lid by slightly tipping the candle over the jar so wax drips onto the lid, or by fastening the candle to the top of the lid by heating the bottom of the candle for a few seconds to melt up the wax and adhering it to the lid. Which method you choose may depend on the size of your jar.

Once the jar is sealed, say slowly and with intention,

I slow down time with this jar of mine.
Seconds lag, and minutes drag,
Make this a case a snail can outpace.
Slow, slow, slow, slow down.

Place your jar spell in the back of your freezer to freeze and slow down time. When you're ready for things to speed up again or resume their normal pace, take the jar out of the freezer and set it in the sun to melt its contents, ending the spell.

JOURNAL QUESTIONS:

How can you use this time to get clearer on your goals and where you're going? In what ways can you practice rest this week? What feelings or emotions come up when you allow the thoughts in your head to quiet?

FIVE OF SWORDS: Let Go of a Grudge

Key words: Conflict, no-win situation, defeat

Sometimes, there's a moment in a fight when you realize that no matter how it ends up, no one will really win. That pit you feel in your stomach when things are over and the regret sets in is a pretty accurate representation of the Five of Swords. The battle is over, lines have been drawn, and if there is a victory on either side, it's a hollow one at best. The Five of Swords teaches that forgiveness and release are the best ways to move forward in these cases.

Five of Swords

A Sweetening Spell for Sour Situations

Timing: Full moon

It'll be tough to move on until you allow yourself to let go of the hard feelings. In this spell, you'll work with the Five of Swords to let go of a grudge.

What you need:

- Paper and pen
- Small bowl
- 5 sour cherries
- Fork
- 1 tablespoon (13 g) sugar
- 1 cup (235 ml) full moon water (see page 31)
- Clear quartz crystal
- Five of Swords tarot card

On a piece of paper, write down the name of the person you've found yourself holding a grudge against, and place the paper in the bottom of the bowl.

Place the five sour cherries, symbolic of the Five of Swords, in the bowl and mash them over the paper with a fork. Sour cherries are bitter, corresponding to bitter feelings felt when holding a grudge. Mashing them over the name paper represents the bitterness felt toward that person.

Sprinkle sugar on top of the mashed sour cherries, in five counterclockwise circles, to sweeten the bitterness. With each circle say,

I release this grudge and all bitter feelings.

Retrieve your full moon water and pour it into the bowl. Full moon water contains properties of release and a great deal of moon energy to aid in your spellwork.

Place the clear quartz crystal in the bowl to aid in absorbing negative energy. Spend some time here and reflect on why you want to cast this spell and how it will help you move forward in a more aligned way. Study the Five of Swords card: How do the figures look? Can you relate to any of them?

Practice deep breathing and visualization for a few minutes: With every breath out, you are exhaling negative energy that no longer serves your greatest good.

Once you feel the grudge and resentment leaving your body, remove the clear quartz crystal and dump the contents of the bowl in the trash to let go of the grudge. Cleanse your clear quartz crystal before using it again.

JOURNAL QUESTIONS:

How has your ego contributed to the grudge you're holding? What is your reaction to conflict? Do you ever feel like you need to cheat to get ahead? If so, why?

SIX OF SWORDS: Release Emotional Baggage

Key words: Leaving things behind, walking away, transition

Has that emotional baggage you've been carrying around given you back pain? Ready to let it go and move on with your life? The Six of Swords represents a time of transition in life, where you're carrying baggage with you into the future. But you can choose to bring the lessons and wisdom and leave behind the heavier things holding you down and back.

 Six of Swords

A Ritual Spell to Let Go of What's Holding You Back

Timing: Full moon, waning moon, or midnight

In this spell, you'll work with the Six of Swords to release emotional baggage. Note: Release is one of the more difficult intentions to work through with your magick. Give yourself ample time to cast this spell, and execute each step with intention. Stop for reflection as needed.

What you need:

- Old suitcase you're willing to part with (a small travel bag from a thrift store works well)
- Six of Swords tarot card
- Lapis lazuli crystal
- Significators of what you're seeking to release (e.g., a letter from an ex, a photo of a person, a relic from childhood, a rejection letter, a blacked-out mirror for poor self-image)
- ½ cup (18 g) rose petals (fresh or dried)
- 1 tablespoon (3 g) rosemary (fresh or dried)
- 1 tablespoon (15 g) salt
- 6 whole cloves
- Paper and pen
- Lighter or matchbook
- Small cauldron or fireproof bowl

Cleanse the suitcase using smoke, sound, and/or crystals to remove all previous energy (see page 13).

Place the Six of Swords tarot card on your work space and visualize yourself in this space of transition. What are you moving away from? What are you moving toward? What are you carrying with you that you don't want to bring into the next phase of your life?

Place the crystal, for release, confidence, and peace, in your pocket.

Inside the suitcase, place the significators of the baggage you're seeking to release. Visualize their energy transferring from your body into the suitcase through a beam of white light.

Sprinkle in the rose petals, to send these things away with love, rosemary, an herb associated with release, and salt, which aids in cleansing and healing. Add the cloves, to represent the Six of Swords, as well as clove's property of driving away negative energy.

Write a goodbye letter to the baggage you're releasing, including why you're ready to let go. Sign and date your name at the bottom. Carefully light the letter on fire and place it in a small cauldron to burn. It's okay if it doesn't burn all the way.

Pour the cooled ash and remaining bits of your goodbye letter over the contents of the suitcase and close it. Take the suitcase and drive until you find a trash bin near a crossroads. Dispose of your baggage. Right before you throw it away, say,

I release this baggage here and now,
It no longer holds me down.
I am weightless, free, and light,
My future looks so very bright.

In magick, crossroads are associated with new directions and possibilities; you're changing the direction of your life and inviting a fresh start.

Keep the crystal with you. Hold on to it and remember your spell if you feel the past creep in.

JOURNAL QUESTIONS:

How has holding on to this baggage affected your ability to move forward? What are you looking forward to in the next chapter of your life? Are there any positives or strengths you've gained from the situations that brought on the baggage?

SEVEN OF SWORDS: Smash
Away Imposter Syndrome

Key words: Cunning, deceit, getting away with something

The Seven of Swords is a card of lies, trickery, deceit . . . and imposter syndrome. If you've been doubting your abilities lately, you may be feeling like you *are* really a fraud. But babe, you're not! Isn't it exhausting to continue the imposter syndrome track playing on a loop in your brain? Let's get rid of it!

Seven of Swords

A *Cathartic Poppet Spell*

Timing: Tuesday

I'll tell you one thing . . . *no one* is lying to you more than that inner voice, telling you to doubt yourself. In this spell, you'll work with the Seven of Swords to smash away imposter syndrome.

What you need:

- Oven-bake clay (black preferred)
- Toothpick or safety pin
- Paper and pen
- Lighter or matchbook
- Purple tea candle
- Seven of Swords tarot card
- Safety glasses
- Hammer

Begin with five to ten minutes of meditation as you reflect on the imposter syndrome you're experiencing. Picture your imposter. Give them a name. What do they look like? What do they say to you? How have they held you back?

Using the clay, make a poppet of your imposter; a poppet is a figure made to represent someone and used in magick and spellcasting. It doesn't have to be detailed, but picture your imposter as you form the shape from clay. Charge the clay with the energy of your imposter as you visualize the imposter energy leaving your body and melding into the clay. Carve their name into the clay with a toothpick. Bake the clay imposter poppet according to the package directions.

While the poppet's baking, light a purple tea candle, for empowerment and confidence, and reflect on the Seven of Swords tarot card. Record your thoughts and answers to the Journal Questions.

Once your imposter poppet has baked and cooled, take it outside, along with safety glasses and a hammer. When you feel ready, put on the safety glasses and smash the imposter poppet with the hammer. Let your emotions take the driver's seat for a moment and get out frustration, fear, anger, sadness . . . whatever you're feeling as you smash away your imposter. See the broken pieces as all of your doubts and fears being smashed away.

Gather the imposter poppet pieces and blow its dust East, the direction of Air, the element associated with the suit of Swords. Air is also associated with clarity; by removing imposter syndrome from the equation, you're getting to the truth of who you are.

Throw the rest of the pieces of your imposter poppet in the garbage where they belong!

When you feel the stinging thoughts of imposter syndrome, recall the name of your imposter poppet and picture smashing and throwing it away. You can also save a few pieces of the imposter poppet and, when you feel imposter syndrome creeping back in, smash a piece to remind yourself who you are!

JOURNAL QUESTIONS:

Why do you feel undeserving of your accomplishments? What evidence do you have that you're successful? What would you tell your best friend if they told you they were dealing with imposter syndrome? Can you apply that same kindness to yourself?

EIGHT OF SWORDS: Free Yourself from Your Shadow

Key words: Feeling trapped, restricted, imprisoned

Right now, your life is filled with a lot of "I can't" energy. Babe, who the f*ck says you can't?! The Eight of Swords illustrates feeling trapped or imprisoned, unable to see what's in front of you or move forward. The sneaky thing is that the swords you're feeling trapped by aren't really trapping you at all. The illusion of imprisonment is keeping you stuck. Sometimes it feels safer to stay small, but what would happen if you trusted yourself and played big?

Eight of Swords

A Mirror Spell for Freedom

Timing: Dusk

Break free of what you *think* is holding you back. In this spell, you'll work with the Eight of Swords to free yourself from your shadow.

What you need:

- Large mirror (floor length or bathroom mirror)
- Lighter or matchbook
- Black chime candle and holder
- Peppermint oil (diluted)
- Eight of Swords tarot card
- Sandalwood incense and holder
- Dry-erase marker
- Eraser

This spell works best with a floor-length mirror that you can sit in front of. You could also sit on your bathroom counter in front of the mirror.

Light the black chime candle and set it in a safe place (preferably near the mirror). Dim the lights in your room. Black is a color associated with shadow work, which is what you are working on in this spell.

Place a small dab of diluted peppermint oil on your forehead for awakening and clarity. This is, in a sense, removing the blindfold from the figure in the Eight of Swords. Set the Eight of Swords card in its reversed position next to, or leaning against, the mirror, symbolically slipping the blindfold from her head. Light the sandalwood incense; one property of sandalwood is aiding in freedom.

Grab the dry-erase marker and get in a comfortable seated position in front of the mirror. Think of eight things that are holding you back or that you're feeling trapped by. These can also be limitations you're placing on yourself. For example, "I'm worried I won't make enough money," "Not good enough," "Failure," "My weight," "It's too late in my life to go after what I want." Write each one across your reflection in black dry-erase marker on a separate line. Begin with writing the first of your eight "swords" across the top of your head in your reflection. Work down, writing one "sword" on a separate line until you reach the bottom of your reflection.

Take a moment to look at your reflection. See how you're holding yourself back with these false narratives or opinions of yourself. When you feel ready, pick up the eraser and read the first line out loud. After you've read it aloud, say,

I free myself from this bind,
This sword imprisoning me is no longer mine.

Erase the words in the first line. Visualize your self-imposed sword prison disappearing.

Repeat this process with each sword line until they are completely gone, and you've freed yourself from the prison.

JOURNAL QUESTIONS:

Why are you keeping yourself small or allowing yourself to remain imprisoned? What have you been telling yourself that you can't do? What is one step you can take to begin to remove the restraints you've placed on yourself or that have been placed on you?

NINE OF SWORDS: Ease
Your Anxiety

Key words: Anxiety, mental anguish, stress

We all know the feeling: that pit in your stomach that causes you to toss and turn and lose sleep as you sweat while your heart races and your muscles tense up . . . those anxious thoughts feel like (nine) stabbing swords. Anxiety can be a real B. This is a card of stress, worry and, yep, anxiety. The Nine of Swords asks you to stop overthinking (easier said than done, I know!) and trust in the Universe. Creating something and pairing it with a semi-repetitive task is the perfect recipe for helping ease those anxious thoughts.

Nine of Swords

A Bracelet Spell to Ease Your Mind

Timing: Monday

You've continually worried about something and the self-talk in your head is looped on negative feedback, leading to more worry and sleepless nights. Give yourself something else to focus on and lose your thoughts in for a few minutes. In this spell, you'll work with the Nine of Swords to create a bracelet to ease your anxiety.

What you need:

- Toothpick or safety pin
- Light blue chime candle and holder
- Vanilla essential oil (diluted)
- Lavender essential oil (diluted)
- Stretchy cord or string
- Scissors
- Black onyx crystal beads
- Nine of Swords tarot card
- Lighter or matchbook
- Small bowl of salt

Begin the spell by taking three deep breaths. With each inhale, visualize warm, calm, glowing energy entering your body. With each exhale, visualize dark, murky anxiety leaving.

Using a toothpick or safety pin, carve the affirmation "I am safe" into your light blue chime candle; light blue is associated with soothing and calm. Anoint the candle with vanilla and lavender oils, for comfort, stress relief, and uplifting energy, by rubbing them on the candle from the top down, three times.

Measure and cut the cord to the approximate size of your wrist, adding a few extra inches for security as you do your spell. String the black onyx crystal beads onto the cord to make a bracelet. Black onyx is associated with grounding, emotional balance, protection, and absorbing negative energy, and is an ideal stone to work with when you feel overwhelmed by anxiety.

Let your mind get lost in the repetition of the beading process. Put on some music you can sing along to as you bead, if you like. Once you have made your bracelet as long as you'd like, knot the ends together three times and say with each knot,

One for grounding,
Two to keep anxiety at bay,
Three for calm,
Anxiety, go away.

Light the candle and let it burn down as you reflect on the Nine of Swords card and journal on the questions with this spell.

Wear your bracelet for calm and grounding and allow your fingers to run over and fidget with the beads when you feel anxious. Mix a few drops of vanilla oil in a small bowl of salt and charge the bracelet in the mixture overnight after you have worn it, to clear the negative energy away.

JOURNAL QUESTIONS:

What physical sensations or changes in your body do you notice when you begin to feel anxiety? What is your main source of worry right now? What thoughts can bring you peace in this moment?

TEN OF SWORDS: Rise from the Ashes

Key words: Painful endings, death, closing one door to open the next

The Ten of Swords is a card of painful endings and closing out a chapter of your life. Although the Ten of Swords is one of the heavier and more uncomfortable cards in the deck, there's also a sense of peace and calm that comes with knowing that something is finally over. It hurts, yes, but now you can begin to heal and move on. It's a great card to reflect on when you're experiencing pain and trauma, as it foretells hope on the other side of pain.

Ten of Swords

A Ritual Spell for Rebirth

Timing: New moon, full moon, or Sunday

The Ten of Swords is reminiscent of a phoenix rising from the ashes–it needs to die in order to be reborn. In this spell, you'll work with the Ten of Swords to rise from the ashes, like a phoenix.

What you need:

- Full-length mirror
- Outfit, makeup, accessories, etc., that make you feel powerful and edgy
- Playlist of empowering songs about rebirth
- Lighter or matchbook
- Red chime candle and holder
- Orange chime candle and holder
- Yellow chime candle and holder
- Dragon's blood incense and holder
- Picture of your past self (who you are rebirthing)
- Small cauldron or fireproof bowl
- Small bowl of new moon water (see page 31)
- Ten of Swords tarot card
- Red or orange feather

This spell is best done in a dark and quiet room, sitting in front of a standing mirror. Put on the outfit you have chosen. Turn on your playlist of empowering songs about rebirth.

Light the candles; the colors represent the flames of rebirth and the flames of the phoenix.

Set each candle in a holder and place them in front of your mirror. Use the flames to light the dragon's blood incense, used for healing and ritual practice.

Choose a picture of your past self, the one who has died and is now being rebirthed as your current self. It can be a picture of you before a heartbreak, trauma, or major life event, for example. Study the picture and reflect on how you've evolved. Speak aloud your goodbye to your past self.

When you feel ready, carefully light the picture on fire, signifying the burning of your past self and rebirth in the flames. Drop the picture in the cauldron to let it burn. It's okay if it doesn't burn all the way.

Pour a small amount of the ashes into your bowl of new moon water, representing new beginnings. Swirl the ashes in a circle three times counterclockwise with your finger.

Remove your finger from the bowl and wipe the ash water on top of your cheeks and down the center of your face, from forehead to chin (the water should be clear), looking down as you do so.

Slowly, raise your head and look at yourself in the mirror. You are reborn from the ashes of your past self: more powerful, resilient, loving, and wise.

Study the Ten of Swords card. What emotions come up? Journal through them. Drip wax from the candles onto your feather and sprinkle the remaining cooled ash from your photo into the hot wax. Once dried, place the feather on your altar to signify your rebirth.

JOURNAL QUESTIONS:

What does this ending mean for you? When was another time in your life that you experienced a painful ending? How did you handle it? What qualities, traits, or attributes are you going to focus on within yourself after this rebirth?

PAGE OF SWORDS: Do Well on a Test

Key words: Communication, quick thinking, sharp intellect

Have one too many cram sessions got you seeing cross-eyed? Nothing can break your spirit or shatter your confidence quite like studying for exams or a test. Suddenly you're questioning your ability, and panic is just around the corner. But before you cross over into full-on dismay, try some tarot magick! Quick-witted, sharp on their feet, and a good communicator, the Page of Swords is chatty and intelligent, great to work with and channel when you want to do well on a test.

Page of Swords

A Sigil Spell for Test Taking

Timing: Morning

Spells for exams and good grades aren't about helping you magically know the answer. They help you trust in your ability to successfully communicate your knowledge. In this spell, you'll work with the Page of Swords to do well on a test. This spell is best done while studying, a day or two before your test.

What you need:

- Lighter or matchbook
- Orange chime candle and holder
- Page of Swords tarot card
- Textbook or notes for the test
- Peppermint essential oil (diluted)
- Paper and pen
- 1 teaspoon ground cinnamon
- Sodalite crystal

Light the orange chime candle, for intelligence, success, and adaptability. Hold the Page of Swords card in your hands and spend a minute or two gazing into the flame, focusing on your intention for the spell. Set the Page of Swords card on top of your textbook or notes to integrate confident communication into your studies while you complete the rest of the spell.

Dab diluted peppermint essential oil, for alertness and awakening, on your forehead, wrists, and the bottoms of your feet.

Using your paper and pen, create a sigil for doing well on your test (see page 18). On a clean sheet of paper, draw your sigil in the middle. Encircle the sigil in the words, "I did great on this test," or whatever phrase feels aligned for you, starting at the top, until you circle back around. Using the past tense when manifesting signifies to the Universe that you've already completed something successfully and aids in drawing its energy to you more effectively.

Sprinkle cinnamon for success on your sigil and place the sodalite crystal in the center. Sodalite aids in communicating effectively. Drip orange wax over the ingredients to seal everything together and then fold the paper until it becomes small enough to fit in your pocket. Be sure to fold the paper toward yourself, to draw the sigil's energy toward you.

Carry the spell with you in your pocket when you take the test. If you can, discreetly draw the sigil somewhere on the test paper to further activate its powers. If you're not able to draw on your test with a pen or pencil, use your finger. Reach into your pocket and hold the spell in your hand when you need extra reassurance during your test.

JOURNAL QUESTIONS:

What subjects are you very knowledgeable in? When was a time that you had to defend what you know or believe in to others? What is your communication style?

KNIGHT OF SWORDS:
Achieve Your Goal

Key words: Success, inspired action, ambition

You're a witch on a mission, and nothing is going to stop you! The Knight of Swords is a card of ambition, action, movement, and success. The energy can be infectious and intoxicating, as you become determined to see things through to the end. Remember, though, you've got to meet the Universe halfway, babe! This spell serves as a source of inspiration. *You* are the one responsible for making your goals come to life!

 Knight of Swords

A Vision Board Mini-Altar Spell

Timing: New moon or Thursday

In this spell, you'll work with the Knight of Swords to achieve your goal by helping you home in on your vision and get excited about taking the steps to achieve it.

What you need:

- Empty shoebox
- Old magazines or printed pictures
- Crafting supplies (scissors, markers, glitter, stickers)
- Glue
- Water from a moving source (river, ocean, creek) in a small bowl
- 1 tablespoon (3 g) dried rosemary
- ¼ teaspoon lemon juice
- Dried bay leaf
- Knight of Swords tarot card
- Smoky quartz

Focus on your goal and spend a few minutes journaling: What do you want to achieve? What will it feel like when you do? What is your motivation? Get crystal clear on these things.

You'll be creating a mini altar or vision board with a shoebox. In the end, the shoebox will sit on its side with the opening facing outward. Find or create pictures that resonate with your goal and glue them on the inside bottom of the shoebox. Add any words or elements you wish, such as glitter, stickers, or ribbon! Take your time and get creative here. Set your decorated altar aside to dry.

Take the bowl of water and set it in front of you. Water from a moving source contains properties of movement, power, and high energy, exactly the properties that are ideal to embody when working to achieve your goals!

Add the rosemary to the bowl, for strength and success, lemon juice for invigoration, and a bay leaf for manifestation, creating a success elixir. Stir the water clockwise with your finger to draw in its energy.

Set your altar up where you will see it and be reminded to work toward your goals. Inside, set the Knight of Swords card, to embody its energy. Place the small bowl of success elixir inside the altar along with the smoky quartz crystal, for success and the courage to tackle your dreams.

When you are taking inspired action toward your goal, remove the smoky quartz, give it a quick dunk in the success elixir, and keep it with you as a talisman of success. Cleanse and replace the crystal once you have finished with it for the day.

Challenge yourself to take one small step toward your goal every day. Stop at your mini altar at least once a day to check in with your progress and keep up motivation.

JOURNAL QUESTIONS:

Why do you want to achieve this goal? What is your inspiration? What could stop you from achieving this goal? How do you plan on handling that obstacle? How will achieving this goal lead you closer to embodying your highest self?

QUEEN OF SWORDS: Strengthen Personal Protection

Key words: Direct, honest, communicative

If there's one situation the Queen of Swords would truly excel in, it would be an awkward holiday family dinner. Many who practice magick are highly empathic, and we tend not to speak up when a relative says something offensive. We brush off personal and probing questions that are asked at a table full of people. The Queen of Swords would be *in her zone*, speaking her truth on conversation topics, shutting down questions she doesn't want to answer by upholding her boundaries, and feeling confident as hell in herself while doing so. Whatever she's drinking, I want some of that!

Queen of Swords

A Mirror Spell for Strength and Boundaries

Timing: Waxing moon or Tuesday

The Queen of Swords is direct, honest, and firm in upholding her boundaries and empowered in her decision-making. In this spell, you'll work with the Queen of Swords to strengthen your personal protection so you can feel confident AF like the Queen herself. This spell also works well for strengthening your personal boundaries and being firm in upholding them while speaking your truth.

What you need:

- Paper and pen
- Black permanent marker
- Compact mirror with mirrors on both inside sides
- Sprinkle of dried basil
- Silver ribbon or wire
- Lighter or matchbook
- Sandalwood incense and holder
- Bowl
- 13 nails
- Queen of Swords tarot card

Focus on what aspect of your life you're seeking to strengthen personal protection in and create a sigil for that on a piece of paper (see page 18).

Once your sigil has been created, draw it in permanent black marker for longevity and staying power on one mirror inside the compact mirror. On the other mirror, draw a pentagram. Pentagrams are symbols of protection that invoke the five elements: Earth, Air, Water, Fire, and Spirit.

Drawing your sigil and pentagram on a mirror will amplify the strength of these symbols and reflect back any bad or negative energy.

Sprinkle a little dried basil over the sigil. Basil is often used for protection and shielding negative energies.

Close your mirror and seal it shut by tying a silver ribbon or wire around it in the shape of an X. Use ribbon for lighter to moderate protection or wire for more heavy-duty protection.

Light the sandalwood incense, for protection, and run the mirror through the incense, charging it with sandalwood's protective properties. As you pass it through the smoke, say,

My walls are reinforced and not easily broken,
Protection comes to life once spoken.
Unwanted energy may not enter or interfere,
My energy is safe when this charm is near.

Set the mirror to charge overnight in a bowl of thirteen nails and the Queen of Swords card.

Keep your personal protection charm with you when you need backup for your boundaries. For extra protection, you can also write your sigil on your body with soap, lotion, or oil before you begin your day.

JOURNAL QUESTIONS:

Do you believe in your personal power? Why or why not? Do you feel uncomfortable confronting or being honest with others? How do you feel when others are honest with you? Do you take things too personally?

KING OF SWORDS: Get Your Question Answered

Key words: Directness, truth, mental clarity

The King of Swords would likely be a man of few words (if he could talk). He is direct, to the point, and honest, and values the truth above all else. He rules more with his head than his heart, although he takes care to make balanced and fair decisions. When faced with a question that's burning at your mind and pulling at your heart, it tends to be hard to find your true answer. Working with the King of Swords is ideal any time you have a question and you're ready to be slapped in the face with the cold, hard truth.

King of Swords

A Scrying Spell to Get Answers

Timing: Full moon or Wednesday

You'll work with the King of Swords to get your question answered, but remember that multiple truths and answers can exist simultaneously! This spell finds the truth or answer that's most aligned with you and the good of your highest self.

What you need:

- Bell
- Full moon water (cooler than room temperature; see page 31)
- Black bowl
- Silver chime candle and holder
- Toothpick or safety pin
- Lighter or matchbook
- King of Swords tarot card
- Paper and pen
- Optional: zip-top bag

Full moon water is ideal to use in this spell, as the full moon acts like a giant cosmic spotlight, highlighting things we should be aware of or might not otherwise see.

Use the bell to cleanse the water, bowl, and silver chime candle. Ring the bell loudly and clearly over each tool and say,

It is clear, the answer is here.

Dim the lights in your room and pour the full moon water into the bowl. Using a toothpick or safety pin, carve "the answer," into the candle. Silver is the color of the King of Sword's sword and is associated with clarity, communication, and intuition.

Light the candle and let it burn for a few minutes. As the candle burns, hold the King of Swords card and call on him to aid you in your quest for an answer. You can also call on your ancestors, deities, or other guides.

Visualize a glowing violet light at the top of your crown, your intuition and spiritual connection, open and receptive, helping you find your answer.

Once sufficient wax has been melted, carefully tilt it over the bowl of moon water and drip the wax into the bowl as you focus intently on your question. Drip as much or as little as you like, for as long a time or short a time as you want. Extinguish the candle and place it in a holder.

Study the wax. What do you see? Look for numbers, letters, figures, shapes, animals, and objects. Let your intuition guide you and write down what you find.

If you're feeling stumped, scoop up the wax drippings and put them in a zip-top bag. Sleep with the bag under your pillow for the answer to be revealed in your dreams. Study the wax for symbols or signs the next morning.

JOURNAL QUESTIONS:

What is your personal truth? Do you lead more with your head or your heart? Could anything be clouding your judgment regarding the answer you're seeking?

ACE OF PENTACLES: Become a Money Magnet

Key words: Manifestation, abundance, new opportunities

Cha-ching, babe! The Ace of Pentacles is a gift from the heavens, offering you abundance and new opportunity. The suit of Pentacles often indicates money or financial matters, and luckily for you when the Ace of Pentacles pops up it tends to be a change for the better for your bank account. Sometimes fear can hold you back, though, so when working with this card for money manifestation, it's important to make yourself extra magnetic to help bust through fears and blocks. Whatever you're looking for in life is looking for you, too, if only you allow yourself to reach out and take it.

Ace of Pentacles

A Magnet Magick Spell for Abundance

Timing: Waxing moon

The Ace of Pentacles is a reminder that abundance is ever present and always accessible to you. In this spell, you'll work with the Ace of Pentacles to become a money magnet.

What you need:
- Coin
- Ace of Pentacles tarot card
- Small square of wax paper
- Pen
- Small magnet
- 1 teaspoon honey
- Small piece of green string

Place your coin on the Ace of Pentacles tarot card, directly over the pentacle. Hold both hands over the card and visualize your wallet or bank account overflowing with money. Leave the coin to charge on top of the card.

At the top of your wax paper, write, "I am a money magnet." Directly below it, write the same sentence, leaving off the last letter, centered underneath the first, creating a descending triangle with your words, to draw money to you. Continue doing this until the last line has only the word "I." It should look like this:

I am a money magnet
I am a money magne
I am a money magn
I am a money mag
I am a money ma
I am a money m
I am a money
I am a mone
I am a mon
I am a mo
I am a m
I am a
I am
I a
I

Each time you write a line, say the full sentence, "I am a money magnet," aloud.

Place the magnet in the center of the wax paper. Place a drop of honey on top of it to sweeten your spell. Put your charged coin on top of the magnet and honey to bind them together, creating a money magnet.

Fold up the wax paper around the money magnet, folding the wax paper toward yourself and turning it clockwise after each fold, to draw money to you.

Finish by tying up the wax paper money magnet with a green string; the color green is associated with money. Keep the spell in your wallet to become a money magnet.

JOURNAL QUESTIONS:

How can you get more creative with ways to attract money to you? Do you *truly* believe that abundance is unlimited and always accessible to you? Why or why not? Is fear holding you back from seizing an opportunity? Why or how?

TWO OF PENTACLES: Stabilize Your Finances

Key words: Balance, adaptation, juggling finances

If the tarot deck is a circus (just go with me here), then the Two of Pentacles is the juggler standing outside the tent, impressing passersby with his seamless ability to keep multiple balls in the air at once. The Two of Pentacles possesses some of the most enviable qualities in the deck: the ability to juggle multiple things at once, time management, and prioritization. If only we were all so skilled! Luckily for you, the Two of Pentacles is here to lend a hand.

Two of Pentacles

An Elemental Spell to Balance Finances

Timing: Noon

The suit of Pentacles often deals with money matters. When this guy pops up, he's a little nudge from the Universe to pay attention to your finances and work to get things manageable. In this spell, you'll work with the Two of Pentacles to balance your finances.

What you need:

- Financial signifier (e.g., printed bank statement, blank check, ATM receipt)
- Red chime candle and holder
- Lighter or matchbook
- Small bowl of water
- Handful of dirt
- Pyrite crystal
- Two of Pentacles tarot card

Hold your financial signifier in both hands and thank the Universe for the abundance in your life. Say aloud, "I thank you, Universe, for my abundance. I now ask for stability and balance in my finances." As you say this, tear or cut your signifier in half, as close to the middle as possible.

Place the two pieces of your signifier on your work space about 12 inches (30 cm) apart from each other.

Place your candle on top of the left piece, and light it. On top of the right piece, place the small bowl of water. You've placed opposing elements–Fire and Water–on your signifier to balance each other out.

Scatter a small line of dirt horizontally across your work space, connecting the two elements. Dirt represents Earth, the element associated with the suit of Pentacles, and is also grounding and stabilizing.

Place the pyrite in the middle of the dirt, creating a center of stability and practicality in your spell.

Place the Two of Pentacles card directly above the pyrite and say,

Balanced now, through and through,
Stabilize my finances, Pentacles of Two.
What's been rocky, is now water still,
A steady flame, and grounded Earth,
Stabilized finances, this is my will.

As the candle burns, visualize what financial balance means to you. Once the candle has burned out, bury the pyrite at a crossroads to complete the spell and stabilize your finances.

JOURNAL QUESTIONS:

Do you spend money emotionally? What coping mechanisms can you practice rather than spending? Where can you pull back your spending more? What is one thing you want to save for? How much money can you set aside for that?

THREE OF PENTACLES: Increase Workplace Harmony

Key words: Teamwork, collaboration, common goals

Sometimes your cosmic report card reads, "Does not play well with others," under the job section. And maybe it's not even your fault! Many personality types in one workplace can be tough to navigate. The Three of Pentacles teaches you that everyone brings something unique to the table, and that if you're able to put your ego aside, you'll be able to work together to achieve great things. Easier said than done, though, amiright?

Three of Pentacles

An Office Supply Spell for the Workplace

Timing: Monday or Wednesday

Whatever your role is at your workplace, if things are feeling shaky with your coworkers, it's time to use your magick to help regroup and work together as a team. In this spell, you'll work with the Three of Pentacles and use a common workplace item, the paper clip, to increase workplace harmony.

What you need:

- Paper and pen
- Three of Pentacles tarot card
- Sticky note
- Purple pen
- 3 paper clips
- Lavender cord or string, 12 inches (30 cm) long

On a piece of paper, create a sigil for harmony in your workplace (see page 18). Study the Three of Pentacles card and see what emotions come up as you create your sigil. Once perfected, draw the sigil on your sticky note with a purple pen, using purple for increasing peace.

Take the three paper clips, to represent the three pentacles, and attach them to the top of your sigil sticky note. Paper clips can be used magickally for binding and bringing things together.

Thread the lavender cord through the top of the paper clips, creating a small banner.

Hang the banner near your desk or work space. When you hang it, say,

A peaceful workplace this will be,
With paper clips and pentacles three,
Bring to this space harmony.

When you're feeling frustrated, take a moment to connect with your sigil and remember your intention of increasing workplace harmony.

JOURNAL QUESTIONS:

How can you better contribute to a more harmonious workplace? When collaborating, do you take on the role of a leader or follower? What unique gifts and talents do you bring to the table?

FOUR OF PENTACLES: Release
Money Insecurity

Key words: Having a tight grip, insecurity, control

When you're feeling like you're about to lose control of something, what's the first thing you do? Tighten your grip on it. Energetically, the tighter we hold on to something, the less space we give it to flow and to receive. The Four of Pentacles indicates holding on tightly to resources, potentially out of fear of losing them. As the suit of Pentacles often relates to money and finances, this card can represent having a tight-knuckle grip on your wallet.

Four of Pentacles

A Clay Shaker Spell for Money Magick

Timing: Full moon or Thursday

Rather than knowing that the Universe will always provide, you're so worried about money that you're clinging to it with an energy of fear of loss. In this spell, you'll work with the Four of Pentacles to help release money insecurity so you can tap into a state of abundance.

What you need:

- Oven-bake clay (green if available, but any color will work)
- Four of Pentacles tarot card
- Pen
- Sprinkle of dried mint
- Sprinkle of dried thyme
- Sprinkle of dried rosemary
- 4 coins
- Toothpick or safety pin

Preheat your oven to the temperature called for on the package of clay. This spell will require you to write on and tear up the Four of Pentacles card; print, photocopy, or draw a picture of the card if you do not want to use the one from your deck.

Turn your Four of Pentacles card upside down, so the imagery looks as if the pentacles will fall away. On the reversed card, write, "Abundance lives within me. The Universe always provides. I release my money insecurities." Rip up the card into small pieces to release your words into the Universe.

Hold the clay in your hands to warm it up. As you manipulate and soften the clay, visualize your energy softening and opening, releasing worry and receiving abundance. Once the clay has softened, sprinkle it with the dried mint and thyme, for money magick, and rosemary for abundance, and work them into the clay.

Create a small bowl with the clay and place the shreds of the Four of Pentacles card inside. Place the four coins, representing money and symbolic of the coins in the Four of Pentacles, on top of the card shreds.

Create a lid and enclose the Four of Pentacles and coins inside the clay, with a hollow space in the middle, pinching the top and bottom together so they don't open, creating a shaker.

Using your toothpick or safety pin, carve "I am abundant" onto the top. You can also draw some dollar signs and pentacles. Bake according to the instructions to seal your spell. By baking coins inside of your clay, you're ensuring that money is always present and available.

Once your clay has baked and cooled, shake your money shaker four times and say aloud,

I know money's always here,
There's no longer a need to fear.
Abundance grows evermore,
I trust there's always more in store.

Abundance is always present and available to you in the form of your money shaker. Give it a shake and repeat the incantation whenever you feel yourself slipping into a lack mind-set around your finances.

JOURNAL QUESTIONS:

What are your current fears around money? Why do you hold the belief that if you release money, it won't come back? In what ways are you already abundant?

FIVE OF PENTACLES: Mend Your Broken Spirit

Key words: Hardship, facing adversity, feeling abandoned

The Five of Pentacles is recognition that things are . . . less than great right now. Feeling alone, abandoned, and like you're constantly climbing uphill can make you feel like you're losing faith. While this is a card of facing adversity, it also offers hope. The Five of Pentacles reminds you that support is there, if only you stop to look around for it and ask.

Five of Pentacles

A Magick First-Aid Spell for Your Spirit

Timing: Monday or Friday

During this time of distress, it's important to take care of yourself and hold the faith that things will take a turn for the better soon. In this spell, you'll work with the Five of Pentacles to mend your broken spirit–the first step for things to start looking up.

What you need:

- Comforting music
- Small rose quartz crystal
- Rose essential oil (diluted)
- Elastic bandage (such as Ace)
- Marker
- Small handheld mirror
- Five of Pentacles tarot card

Play your comforting music and lie down in a comfortable spot, rose quartz in hand. Pillows and blankets are handy to have around for this part, too!

Close your eyes and focus on where things are feeling broken or wounded emotionally. Where do these feelings reside in your body? Hold the rose quartz, associated with love and healing, on those places and visualize its loving and healing energy entering each cell of your body and filling it with a healing glow.

Dab rose essential oil, also for love and healing, on the same places you held the rose quartz.

Using a word or phrase that concerns healing, create a sigil (see page 18). It could be as simple as the word "healed" or the phrase "I am healed," or whatever is resonating with you. Be sure to use present-tense words. Draw the sigil on the elastic bandage, a healing tool, with a marker.

Pick up the handheld mirror and truly look at yourself. Try to see the resilience, strength, and badass witch looking back. Think about all you have overcome; you've made it this far, and you will continue to make it through anything life throws at you.

Place the rose quartz over the mirror and wrap the crystal, Five of Pentacles card, and mirror together with the bandage sigil. Seal it with a kiss to mend your broken spirit.

JOURNAL QUESTIONS:

Have you reached out for help recently? Who can you talk to? Think back to a difficult time: How did you come through the other side? How can you redirect your focus to shift into a mind-set of abundance?

SIX OF PENTACLES: Recover
Money Owed

Key words: Giving and receiving, sharing wealth, balance

There are very few things more awkward in life than trying to recover money from someone who's in debt to you. (*Maybe* that dream where you show up to school in your underwear, but hey, that's just a dream.) While it's natural to go through cycles of being the giver and recipient, it's best to always ensure you're working toward paying back debts to even and clear the energy. A card of giving and receiving, perfectly even scales, and energy moving in a circular motion, the Six of Pentacles represents that stabilized middle we're all aiming for.

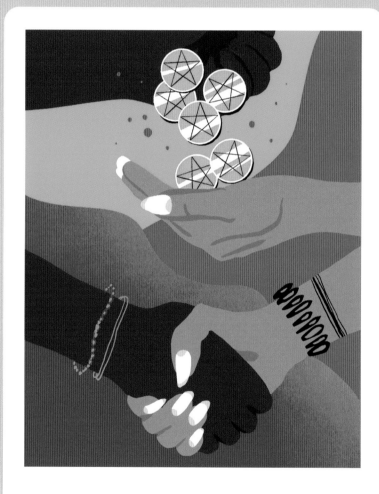

Six of Pentacles

A Candle Magick Spell to Encourage Repayment

Timing: Tuesday

When the scales are thrown off and suddenly that friend you loaned money to stops taking your calls, try this spell. You'll work with the Six of Pentacles to recover money owed.

What you need:

- Photo of person who owes you money
- Black pen
- 6 whole cloves
- Six of Pentacles tarot card
- Dollar bill
- 1 teaspoon cayenne pepper
- Red chime candle
- Toothpick or safety pin
- Lighter or matchbook

On the back of the photo, write out the full name of the person who owes you money, along with their birthdate and the amount of money owed.

Place three cloves, for money manifestation, on each side of the photo. These represent the balance of money being lent and repaid.

Place the Six of Pentacles card, along with a dollar bill, representing money owed, on top of the photo, and sprinkle cayenne atop everything, to impress urgency and haste upon the person who owes you money.

On the red candle, for power and energy, use the toothpick or safety pin to inscribe the amount of money owed. Light the candle and drip a little wax atop the dollar bill.

Set the candle on top of the wax to hold it in place, and let the candle burn for a few minutes as you envision the person paying you back what is owed. Say aloud,

Money owed is now repaid,
Now that this spell is laid.
What is mine, I call back to me,
This debt is repaid hastily.

Extinguish the candle (do not blow it out) and light it while repeating the visualization every night until the person pays you back the money owed.

JOURNAL QUESTIONS:

When was a time you benefited from the generosity of others? In what ways do you provide for and serve your community? What emotions come up when you think of "debt"?

SEVEN OF PENTACLES: Grow Your Business

Key words: Patience, long-term planning, results

Tom Petty and the Heartbreakers sure knew what they were talking about when they sang to us, "The waiting is the hardest part." One of the most difficult parts of working with magick is the patience it takes to actualize your goals. But wait! What happened to overnight success?! When it comes to your business, the Seven of Pentacles teaches that it takes time and investment to yield fruitful and long-lasting results.

 Seven of Pentacles

A *Plant Magick Spell for Business Growth*

Timing: New moon, waxing moon, or Sunday

Tending to your business is a lot like gardening: It takes time and care to get what you're looking for. In this spell, you'll work with the Seven of Pentacles to grow your business and make sure that you're able to see the big picture so you don't pick your fruit prematurely.

What you need:

- Basil plant seeds
- Seven of Pentacles tarot card
- Motivational music playlist
- Clay planter pot
- Tools to decorate clay planter (paint, ribbon, glitter, markers)
- Soil
- 7 pennies
- Small citrine crystal
- Small carnelian crystal
- Small green aventurine crystal

Place the basil seeds, which correspond to money, luck, and business, on top of the Seven of Pentacles card and leave them there to charge.

Put on motivating music and spend time thoughtfully decorating the clay planter. The planter is a representation of your business, so use colors that correspond to your business intentions. Write affirmations along the top. Really get creative!

Once the planter is decorated, add soil. Inside the soil, bury the seven coins, representative of the Seven of Pentacles tarot card, as well as growing financially. Bury the citrine, for abundance, carnelian, for motivation and action, and green aventurine, for prosperity and confidence. Last, add the basil seeds.

Draw a pentacle on top of the soil with your finger and say,

My business grows successfully,
And flourishes with these seeds.
Happiness, achievement, and money come easily.
My business meets all my needs.
Growing business, blooming plant,
Together are one with this chant.

Your plant is a magickal talisman for your business; tend to it thoughtfully and with care. As the weeks and months go on, continue to add magick items to your plant, such as crystals, or stick dollar bills out of the soil, as if growing, and use it to bury intention lists for your business. Once the basil has grown, pick a few leaves to use in manifestation spellwork.

Set the plant in full sun and water once a week. Bring indoors during cold weather.

JOURNAL QUESTIONS:

Where will your business be in six months? One year? What are two things you can do to work toward your long-term vision for your business or goals? What are you willing to invest in your goals?

EIGHT OF PENTACLES: Develop Your Skills

Key words: Apprenticeship, hard work, mastery

There's that old joke, "How do you get to Carnegie Hall? Practice, practice, practice." The fellow in the Eight of Pentacles knows that well. A card that reminds you that repetition is key to developing your craft, the Eight of Pentacles symbolizes hard work, determination, and concentration. Whether you're looking to further skills for your career, personal development, or hey, maybe even to get to Carnegie Hall, the Eight of Pentacles is a card to keep close by.

Eight of Pentacles

A Witch's Ladder Spell for Skill Development

Timing: Night

Remember, it's not about the destination, but about the (detail-oriented and diligently traveled) journey. In this take on the classic witch's ladder spell, you'll work with the Eight of Pentacles to develop your skills.

What you need:

- Light blue cord, about 24 inches (61 cm) long
- Eight of Pentacles tarot card
- 8 gold beads

Reflecting the lesson in the Eight of Pentacles that developing new skills takes repetition to achieve mastery, this spell will have you knot a cord repeatedly as you work your magick.

Hold the light blue cord in one hand. Light blue is for wisdom and knowledge. Hold the Eight of Pentacles card in the other hand as you focus on the skill(s) you seek to develop.

Starting on one end of the cord, tie each gold bead, for illumination, as you say the following incantation out loud. Recite each line as you tie the corresponding bead number into a knot. Visualize yourself with your new skills as you say,

By knot of one, the spell's begun.
By knot of two, my skills are true.
By knot of three, I learn easily.
By knot of four, I open new doors.
By knot of five, my passion will thrive.
By knot of six, errors I fix.
By knot of seven, I absorb all lessons.
By knot of eight, my will be fate.

The next night, untie each bead and repeat the spell again, repeating the entire process (untying the previous night's knots and retying them) for a total of eight nights.

After the eighth night, store the knotted cord in a place that reflects your learning journey (for example, on your desk, bookshelf, or near your computer) to develop your skills.

JOURNAL QUESTIONS:

How willing are you to commit to developing new skills? How well do you finesse details in your work? How might that help or hinder you? Do you consider yourself a hard worker? Why or why not?

NINE OF PENTACLES: Empower Yourself

Key words: Empowerment, success, abundance

Time for some real talk, babe. When was the last time you stopped, looked around, and truly marveled at the amazing witch you are? The Nine of Pentacles is the embodiment of all of those things we *should* be doing and feeling about ourselves: independent, luxurious, abundant, empowered; someone who has worked hard and is unapologetically enjoying the fruits of their labor. Easier said than done, I get it! Good thing you're reading just the book to help you connect with the confident Nine of Pentacles witch within you!

Nine of Pentacles

A Jewelry Charm Spell for Empowerment

Timing: Sunday or Friday

When was the last time you fully owned your accomplishments and spoke of yourself with pride? In this spell, you'll work with the Nine of Pentacles to empower yourself.

What you need:

- Glass of wine or sparkling grape juice
- Lighter or matchbook
- Yellow chime candle and holder
- Piece of gold jewelry
- Nine of Pentacles tarot card
- Orange
- Pen

Pour your glass of wine to sip while you complete your spellwork. This is symbolic of the grapes in the Nine of Pentacles and also a representation of the luxury reflected in the card.

Light a yellow chime candle. Yellow is associated with happiness and self-empowerment and is the main color in the Nine of Pentacles in the Rider-Waite-Smith deck.

Place your gold jewelry on top of the Nine of Pentacles card and peel the orange, which corresponds to energy and joy. Separate the sections of the orange, and with each section, say aloud a word that describes your most Nine of Pentacles self, such as "confident," "bold," "expansive," or "unafraid to take up space," then eat the section of orange, integrating the energy into your physical being.

As you do this, write down each word or phrase on the orange peel.

Once the orange has been eaten, put on the piece of gold jewelry, charged with confidence, power, and embodiment of the Nine of Pentacles, and say,

I embrace my confidence and magickal glow,
Sparkling and golden, empowerment bestow.

Let the orange peel dry out and use it in future spellwork, such as incense or anointing oils that have to do with power, confidence, or self-love. Wear your charged gold jewelry whenever you need an extra boost of self-empowerment.

JOURNAL QUESTIONS:

What makes you feel powerful? List three accomplishments you've achieved this year. When was the last time you celebrated yourself? Are you overdue for it?

TEN OF PENTACLES: Build Lasting Financial Stability

Key words: Strong foundations, financial security, family wealth

A card of solid foundations and lasting family security, the Ten of Pentacles depicts a legacy many hope to leave behind. Your focus right now is on the long game, and how you can work to ensure lasting financial stability for yourself and future generations. If you're not quite there yet, the Ten of Pentacles is a sign of assurance that your hard work will pay off and things will come together eventually. Don't give up!

 Ten of Pentacles

A *Coin and Sigil Spell for Financial Foundations*

Timing: Thursday

Use this time to focus on long-term goals, stay consistent, and hone in on your vision for the future. In this spell, you'll work with the Ten of Pentacles to build lasting financial security.

What you need:

- Money manifesting playlist
- Paper and pen
- Black permanent marker
- 10 ribbons of various colors, about 24 inches (61 cm) long
- Glue
- 1 tablespoon (2 g) dried mint
- 10 coins
- Ten of Pentacles tarot card

Put on your money manifesting playlist and listen to the music as you complete your spellwork.

On a piece of paper, create a sigil (see page 18) using your last name plus the phrase "financial stability." Draw the sigil in permanent marker, for lasting foundations, ten times down each ribbon.

Place a dot of glue on the bottom of the ribbon and sprinkle dried mint, associated with money magick, into the glue. Lay a coin on top to glue it to the bottom of the ribbon. Repeat with each ribbon.

Once the ribbons have dried, place the coin end of each ribbon on top of the Ten of Pentacles card. Hold both hands palm down over them and say,

I charge this spell with lasting financial stability,
And with ten times ten I create this for myself and
  my family.
The future is stable and strong as the tree,
These coins of ten will foresee.

Take your charged coins and hang them in a tree in your yard. Trees are symbolic of grounding and the Earth element, which the suit of Pentacles is associated with. As the tree grows, spreads its roots, and becomes more solid, so does your spell, building lasting financial security.

If you don't have a yard or tree, hang the ribbons in the branches of a plant. (This can be a large plant in your yard or a potted plant inside the house.) Remove the ribbons after ten days and place them on your altar for the manifestation of lasting financial stability.

JOURNAL QUESTIONS:

What is your family money story? How has the way your family handled finances influenced your relationship with money? What do you want to pass down to the next generation?

PAGE OF PENTACLES: Bless Your New Business

Key words: New opportunity, goal focused, manifestation

New beginnings are a' comin'! Maybe you're still in the planning phase, or maybe you've taken the first few steps in your new venture—whatever it is, you've got that excited energy, ready to get going. The Page of Pentacles is a great card to work with when starting a new business; it signifies optimism, opportunity, and manifestation—all of the right spell ingredients for your new business potion.

Page of Pentacles

A Business Blessing Powder Spell

Timing: Sunday or Thursday

You can't bottle up your enthusiasm to help carry you through the difficult times, but you can do the next best thing . . . bottle up a new business blessing powder! In this spell you'll work with the Page of Cups to bless your new business.

What you need:

- Bowl and spoon
- Ground cinnamon
- Ground ginger
- Dried peppermint
- Dried chamomile
- Dried lemon balm
- Crumbled dried bay leaves
- Crushed eggshells for prosperity
- Small square of paper and pen
- Lighter or matchbook
- Small cauldron or fireproof bowl
- Airtight container to store powder
- Small jade crystal
- Coin
- Page of Pentacles tarot card

In a bowl, mix the spices and herbs and crushed eggshells together with a spoon. Let your intuition guide you for how much of each ingredient to add. Remember, this is a spell for *your* unique business, there's no wrong way to do it!

As you add each ingredient, spend a moment to hold it in your hands. Taste it. Connect to it.

Visualize its properties being added to your spell powder.

On your paper, create a success sigil for your business (see page 18) or simply write down your business name. Light the paper on fire and let it burn in a small cauldron. Add the cooled ashes to your powder as a significator for your business.

Transfer your business success powder to an airtight container to store it, and add the jade crystal, for luck and prosperity, and coin, a symbol of the suit of Pentacles.

Close the lid and gently shake everything together as you say,

May this powder bless my business with success.

Place the Page of Pentacles card on top of the container to charge the powder with its energy while it's stored.

Use the new business success powder in spellwork related to your business. Some ideas include dusting important documents, dressing candles for spellwork, or sprinkling it around the workplace to bless your new business with success.

JOURNAL QUESTIONS:

What are you feeling excited about exploring? If you believed in your unlimited potential, what goals would you set for yourself? The Page of Pentacles is an avid learner. Where can you continue your education or expand your knowledge related to your career or business?

KNIGHT OF PENTACLES: Have a Productive Week

Key words: Hard work, persistence, reliability

The Knight of Pentacles is a hardworking, reliable (sometimes boring) knight. He's the guy home on a Saturday night planning his week, while the rest of the knights are out partying. Whenever you need a little kick in the pants to remind you to buckle down and get to business, the Knight of Pentacles is the one to work with. The Knight of Pentacles reminds you that being practical, reliable, and patient is the key to achieving your goals.

Knight of Pentacles

An Earth Magick Spell for Productivity

Timing: Sunday

On days when you just can't seem to focus and get into gear, the Knight of Pentacles is there to help. In this spell, you'll work with the Knight of Pentacles to have a productive week.

What you need:

- Cup of coffee or other beverage (preferably caffeinated)
- Paper and pen
- Handful of dirt
- Plate
- Knight of Pentacles tarot card

As you make your coffee, focus on your intentions for the week and all that you are aiming to get done. Stir clockwise three times to stir your intentions into your drink.

Drink your coffee as you write out your to-do list. Coffee is great to work with for productivity and a boost of energy.

Sprinkle the dirt onto your plate, so there is a light layer covering the entire plate.

Using your finger, draw a pentagram in the dirt. In the Knight of Pentacles card, the dirt is symbolic of the knight's hard work and is also associated with the element of Earth. The pentagram is associated with the suit of Pentacles, and also represents the five elements: Earth, Air, Water, Fire, and Spirit.

Rub your finger in the top point of the pentagram, and then touch it to your forehead and say,

Element of Spirit, this I ask,
Bring me focus and productivity in my task.

Moving clockwise, rub your finger in the right point of the pentagram, touch it to your right palm, and say,

Element of Water, this I ask,
Bring me flow and productivity in my task.

Rub your finger in the lower right point of the pentagram, touch it to the bottom of your right foot, and say,

Element of Fire, this I ask,
Bring me motivation and productivity in my task.

Rub your finger in the lower left point of the pentagram, touch it to the bottom of your left foot, and say,

Element of Earth, this I ask,
Bring me grounding, and productivity in my task.

Rub your finger in the left point of the pentagram, touch it to your left palm, and say,

Element of Air, this I ask,
Bring me clarity of mind and productivity in my task.

The dirt shouldn't really stick to your body, it's more about the transference of energy.

Set your to-do list, along with the Knight of Pentacles card, on top of the dirt pentagram and repeat the spell when needed to have a productive day.

JOURNAL QUESTIONS:

What emotions does the phrase "hard work" bring up for you? Why are you resistant to accomplishing your goals? Is self-sabotage at play? What's motivating you to accomplish your goals or complete your to-do list?

QUEEN OF PENTACLES: Always Have Cash in Your Pocket

Key words: Wealth, financial independence, dependability

The Queen of Pentacles is the mom you turn to when you need advice about your finances. She's practical and will tell it like it is, but is also nurturing and kind. She asks you to be resourceful and quick thinking and to use your unique strengths to problem solve. When you find yourself in a pickle, she's there to bail you out and help you plan more sustainably for the future.

 Queen of Pentacles

A Magick Pocket Spell for Cash

Timing: New moon or Thursday

While you may not always have someone like the Queen of Pentacles in your life, you can create some magick with these same supportive qualities! In this spell, you'll work with the Queen of Pentacles to ensure that you always have cash in your pocket.

What you need:

- The pocket from an old item of clothing
- Cinnamon stick
- Poppy seeds
- $13 in paper bills
- Coin
- Queen of Pentacles tarot card
- Safety pin

Inside the pocket, place a cinnamon stick, to draw money to you, poppy seeds, to represent the continual growth of money, the $13 (the Queen of Pentacles is the thirteenth card in the suit of Pentacles), a coin to represent the suit of Pentacles, and the Queen of Pentacles tarot card, folded toward you three times.

Close the pocket with a safety pin and say,

Queen of Pentacles, always on hand,
Keep cash in my pocket wherever I am.

Keep the magick pocket with you in your wallet, purse, backpack, or car. Use the money when you're in a pinch, and be sure to replace it as soon as you can. Always leave the coin in your pocket so it's never empty.

JOURNAL QUESTIONS:

Do you view money as something that nurtures you, or as a source of problems? Why? How can you show up for yourself financially? (For example, start a savings account, spend less money eating out, invest in your business, etc.), What was your mother's or family's view of money? How has that influenced your money story?

KING OF PENTACLES: Protect Your Money

Key words: Wealth, abundance, success

Are you feeling that the second you make money, it's somehow already slipping out of your hands? Money is coming in, but never quite staying. The King of Pentacles can be looked at as your personal wealth guard: He's practical, confident, and has a keen focus for accumulating and protecting his wealth. He makes decisions that will benefit him in the long run and is picky with his investments.

King of Pentacles

A Wreath Spell for Money Magick

Timing: Full moon or Thursday

A hardworking leader and smart businessman, the King of Pentacles is assured in his self-confidence and his ability to be a financial provider. In this spell, you'll work with the King of Pentacles to protect your wealth.

What you need:

- Garland of grape vines (artificial works best for this)
- Wire wreath frame
- Twist ties (or something to secure the vine to the wreath frame)
- 7 paper money bills of any amount
- 1 teaspoon grapeseed oil
- Green ribbon
- King of Pentacles tarot card
- Small green or gold sachet
- 1 tablespoon (3 g) dried rosemary

Secure your garland of grape vines to the wire wreath frame with twist ties, creating a grape garland wreath. Grapes are symbolic in the King of Pentacles card as a sign of patience, fertility, and wisdom and are commonly used in money magick spells.

Anoint each bill with grapeseed oil, also associated with money magick, by dipping your finger in the oil and drawing a pentagram on each bill.

Roll up the paper bills and tie each one to the grape vine wreath using green ribbon, a color associated with money magick.

Place the King of Pentacles card in a small green or gold sachet to stand guard over your money. Add the rosemary, for protection. Tie the sachet atop the garland.

Hang the wreath in your home and when you are feeling concerned over finances, take a little rosemary from the sachet and blow it to the North for strength to protect your finances.

JOURNAL QUESTIONS:

What is your relationship to self-discipline and finances? How could you feel safer and more secure in your finances? What does your vision of financial success look like?

List of Spells by Subject

PROTECTION

LOVE & RELATIONSHIPS

MONEY

CAREER & SCHOOL

HOME

⬩ Acknowledgments ⬩

My husband, Logan: Thank you for holding down the fort while I embarked on the wild endeavor of writing two books in one year. Every day I'm grateful for your support, love, and encouragement. Maybe this next year I'll slow down a bit (no promises).

My editor, Jill Alexander: Thank you for your continued belief in me and in this book. Your wisdom and support are unparalleled and I'm truly so grateful to work with you.

My developmental editor, Jenna Nelson Patton: You have the ability to make the process feel less like work and more like emailing an old friend. Thanks for always putting a smile on my face with your encouraging notes (that I screenshot and read over again when I'm feeling down).

My mom, Carrie: Thank you for listening to my ideas and always being willing to take my calls and be a sounding board. Also, thanks for introducing me to tarot as a kid . . . who would have thought it would lead us here!

My Cosmic Coven, aka social media community, clients, and friends: You all mean so much to me. Thank you for contributing to an online space that feels like interacting with close witchy friends. Every interaction is appreciated and I'm so grateful for your support.

The original tarot witch, Pamela Colman Smith: Thank you for your contributions to art, the occult, and society. Without you, we would not know and love tarot as we do today.

Bibliography

Cunningham, Scott. *Cunningham's Encyclopedia of Magical Herbs.* 2nd ed. Woodbury, MN: Llewellyn, 2000.

Kynes, Sandra. *Llewellyn's Complete Book of Correspondences.* Woodbury, MN: Llewellyn, 2013.

About the Author

Sam Magdaleno is a professional witch and tarot reader. Creatrix of the popular Instagram handle Sam the Cosmic Witch, Sam offers resources on witchcraft and tarot, as well as a monthly membership centered around working with moon magick. She specializes in demystifying witchcraft and making it practical and applicable to everyday life. Having grown up visiting Wiccan shops and collecting crystals with her mom, Sam experienced the positive influence that witchcraft had on her life and is dedicated to helping others live in alignment with their inner witch. Sam is obsessed with overalls, coffee, and horror movies. She lives in Alberta, Canada.

About the Illustrator

Tanya Jacobson is a designer and illustrator based in Minnesota. You can find her illustration and design work on coffee tables all across the globe including titles *The Thrifty Witch's Book of Simple Spells* and *The Healed Empath*. With more than a decade of accomplished design under her belt, Tanya's award-winning work has been featured in numerous publications, including *Print*, *The Type Directors Club*, *Logo Lounge*, *Communication Arts*, and *HOW*. When she's not creating, you can find her in the woods enjoying the outdoors year-round with her family in northern Wisconsin.

INDEX